Agony In The Garden

THE STORY OF A GAY MINISTER

by

Howard Hannon

OutWrite Publishing
Portland, Oregon

ISBN 1-887092-01-3

To My Grandchildren
Kelle Leber and Charles Leber IV
and
Megan Hannon and Lindsey Hannon

That they may know

ACKNOWLEDGEMENTS

In a very real sense this book was written in true Presbyterian fashion, by committee. After preparing a section of the book I then gave it to different persons from all walks of life for their comments. When they had finished reviewing the material they returned it to me. I accepted their criticisms and suggestions which meant I had to rewrite the material many times.

I thank Mr. Vern Ryles who took time from running his business and his many community involvements to read the material and then discuss what he had read with me. My sister, Joan Wolfarth, responded from the point of view of her training in Christian Education, and her position as the Stated Clerk of a Presbytery. Ed Miller came to be the director of the Day Care in the Coos Bay Presbyterian church in 1972. We discovered each other and our friendship has lasted through the years. He responded as a gay man, and one who observed what was happening in the church when we were in the midst of the lowest point of our journey.

I greatly appreciate Herman Waetjen, professor at San Francisco Theological Seminary, who took time while on sabbatical leave to read the manuscript and give his suggestions and comments. I am most grateful for his writing the forward. I am also indebted to the Rev. Tom Castlen who suggested I write this story. In the early stages of writing it was his criticism which helped me to move from just giving condensations of my sermons to writing my story.

Finally last, but not least, I thank John Rusniak for all he has meant to me in my life and in the writing of the book. Not only did he work with the content of the book, but he functioned as an oasis, a time of refreshment, when the task became difficult and I needed my spirits lifted. In a very real sense this book is the result of this very informal committee, and I thank them all.

PREFACE

This book might also be entitled, "A Gay Presbyterian Minister's Odyssey." This is an account of my life beginning with the awakening of my sexuality and my spiritual life. As I looked back over my life I discovered that these two aspects of my life went hand in hand.

As a young man of high school age I was an ardent fundamentalist. This religious background did not keep me from responding to sexual encounters when approached. Those sexual moments often produced a conflict between satisfying my sexual desires and my religious training which did not allow sex outside marriage. Following a stint in the Army Air Force as a chaplain's assistant, finishing my college education, I enrolled in the San Francisco Theological Seminary. In my studies I was exposed to what is known in Biblical Scholarship as the "Historical - Critical Approach." This freed me from the confines of the fundamentalistic approach, and opened new avenues of understanding the Biblical message. It did not free me from the internal struggle between my sexual and spiritual desires. In seminary I also learned that graduation did not mean I knew it all and continuing education became part of my professional life.

Basically this book is the story of my ministry as the pastor of the First Presbyterian Church of Coos Bay, Oregon. The results of my continuing education while in Coos Bay led me to view the Gospels as confessions of faith, not religious history. Gethsemane, Good Friday and Easter are the culminating events in the life of Jesus, and the Gospels are the response of the different evangelists to that event. Good Friday and Easter are the model for all human lives which means that the Biblical past is also the Biblical present. I did not keep this wonderful knowledge to myself. It was the basis of my preaching and teaching.

There are many people who have been turned off and away from the Christian faith by the institutional church with its quasi-fundamentalist approach. The institutional church and fundamentalist of today outdo the Pharisees of Jesus' day. The message of Jesus was to free the people of his day from the false confines of the Jewish faith, and the approach of this book is to free the reader from the confines of the institutional church of today.

On Sunday January 16, 1966, I began a spiritual trek in the wilderness and the account of that journey is the context of the pages of this book. There are three entwining facets in this journey: my life, the theology given in the sermons (and condensed for this book), and the reaction of the members to that message. As I move from one to the other I have tried to do this in a manner that enables the reader to follow.

Many gay men and lesbian women have looked to the church for support in their spiritual lives, only to find disdain, judgment, condemnation, and a "you are not wanted here" welcome. This may be the message of the institutional churches, but it is not the message of the Bible. Our sexual orientation is a given from the Divine, and only when we accept that given will we find peace within. The world tells us that happiness is the goal of our lives, but in the Gospel of John, Jesus said, "Peace is my parting gift to you, my own peace, such as the world cannot give." (John 14;17)

When this spiritual journey began I felt totally alone. Israel in the Old Testament had a cloud by day, a pillar of fire at night, and footprints in the sand. I felt we, in the Coos Bay Church, did not have any help. I was wrong. As I recalled the events I discovered there had been footprints in the sand leading me, my family, and the congregation through all of the experiences I share with you in the pages which follow.

Howard Hannon
Portland, Oregon

FORWARD

The rule of the Heavens is like a human being who sowed good seed in his field. While the human beings (the farm community) were sleeping, his enemy came and sowed darnels in the middle of the wheat, and he went off. Now when the grass sprouted and made fruit, then the darnels were manifested. And approaching, the slaves of the housemaster said to him, "Master, did you not sow good seed in your field? How then does it have darnels?" And he said to them, "An enemy did this!" The slaves said to him, "Do you wish that we go off and collect them? And he said, "No, lest collecting the darnels you simultaneously uproot the wheat with them. Let both grow together until the harvest. Then in the season of the harvest I will say to the harvesters, 'First collect the darnels and bind them into bundles so that they may be burned, but gather the wheat into my barn.'" (Matthew 13:24-30)

Jesus told stories in order to give his contemporaries a glimpse of the character and conditions of God's rule which he was engaged in actualizing through his ministry. His parables, however, also had another function: to subvert the social construction of reality which the ruling elite had constituted by means of world-building myths. This story, the parable of the wheat and darnels, is a superlative instance of his pedagogical technique. Even as the housemaster refuses to let his slaves rid his wheat field of the noxious darnels by a process of weeding – and insists on postponing the separation until harvest – so the rule of God rejects all efforts at discrimination, all attempts to categorize human beings in order to separate one kind from another kind.

The Judaism of Jesus' day maintained the ideology of separation that was ultimately founded on the Priestly Code's myth of creation. As God had separated light from darkness, so God had also separated the people of Israel from the rest of the world. Intimately linked to the purity code of Leviticus and its subsequent expansion, this ideology of separation established a pollution system that divided the world into the two realms of the sacred and the profane, the clean and the unclean. Jews were clean. Samaritans and Gentiles were unclean. The rich and the healthy were clean, the poor and the sick were unclean.

In telling this parable of the wheat and the darnels, Jesus attacked the pollution system and its ideology of separation. The rule of God which Jesus was commissioned to establish and which Jesus subsequently entrusted to his disciples (Luke 22:29) is not only antagonistic to all pollution systems. It is an active agent at work in the world, like yeast which a woman hides in fifty pounds of flour – to draw upon another parable of Jesus – that is engaged in undermining all institutions, traditions, purity codes and pollution systems that dehumanize and destroy human beings and therefore contradict God's will.

The culture of the United States is profoundly infected with a vast pollution system that generates racism, sexism, classism, misogyny and homophobia. And contrary to God's will and Jesus' teaching, church communities that identify themselves as Christian not only buy into this pollution they legitimate it, they propagate it and thereby facilitate the spread of its poisonous infection throughout society, willfully as well as unconsciously. As a result, Christianity maintains and lives by the same ideology of separation that Jesus confronted in the Judaism of his time.

Here is a forthright story, honest and powerful, a story that may move you to tears – of a Presbyterian minister who after marriage discovers that he is gay and struggles while a husband and a pastor to resolve this terrible existential crisis of his God-given sexuality. Resolutely he gradually affirms his homosexuality and eventually reveals his orientation to the members of his congregation with whom he has been engaged in a theological dialogue of challenge and response for many years. In coming out of the proverbial closet, he realizes the truth of the gospel and through a process of metamorphoses begins to emerge from the cocoon of non-being, like a beautiful butterfly. His wings may still be weak and fluttering, but he has begun to fly.

Herman C. Waetjen
Robert S. Dollar Professor of New Testament
San Francisco Theological Seminary

x

CONTENTS

A PSALM

Clap your hands! Shout for joy!
Let your bodies and voices explode
with the joy of the Christian faith.
"God" is not some human concoction,
some Supreme Being, up there
pulling the strings of our little puppet lives.
All religious attempts to define "God"
will not box him in;
all attempts to rationalize "God" out of existence
will fail.

"God" is the Persistent Agent of Love
which keeps breaking into human life.

The rulers of the nations seek to ignore
this Persistent Love,
which continues to break up their schemes
to keep human beings in bondage.

The masses of people substitute
their own little authorities,
which they call "God,"
and erect their defense mechanisms
against this 'Love.'
But the Persistent Agent of love confronts us all;
in the faces of the hungry children of this world,
in the searching eyes of those made homeless
by the folly of war,
in the hatred of oppression, forced on them by others,
in the pleas for help from the drug addict, the alcoholic,
in the human lives which have been broken
in body, mind and spirit.

In just such human situations
we are confronted by Love,
and we alone can be the Agent who can bring them
comfort, joy, and a new life.

Clap your hands! Shout for joy!
To be Christian is to be
the Agent of Love to those in need.

REMINISCENCES

It is a nice warm July day in Oregon. A great day for wearing shorts and a loose fitting polo shirt. The weatherman has promised hot weather, but I hope I will get to the coast before I have to use the air conditioner in the car. I like warm weather and as I drive to Coos Bay I want to enjoy the warm wind blowing through what little hair still resides on the top of my head. Since I am not in a hurry I will avoid the freeways and take the back roads. I do not like the freeways! They are a bore! They do not take you through the countryside where you have a chance to see the farmlands and appreciate the small towns.

Soon Portland and its suburbs are behind me and I find myself in the wine country. I am in the beginning of Oregon's wine country. Row after row of vines greet my eyes. A railroad runs parallel with the highway. I always enjoy driving next to a railroad. Being an eternal optimist, I hope a train will come along and make my day even better. No luck. I can tell by the condition of the rails that it is a branch line with little traffic. Soon the wine country gives way to a valley, with the coast mountains off to one side and small hills on the other. Here and there I see a dairy farm. Shades of my youth. Many a summer had been spent on my uncle's farm. Memories come flooding back, and I enjoy reliving most of them.

One memory which comes to mind is the summer following my freshman year in high school. The year was 1938. It was Sunday morning and we had all gone to church. Sitting in the pew, I looked up at the choir, and there he was. He saw me. I saw him, and in that look between us, something clicked. I knew I wanted to meet him. After dinner (in those days the main meal of the day was at noon and called dinner) I jumped on my bike and rode into town thinking somehow or other I would find him. Rather foolish on my part. I did not know him from Adam and I did not have the foggiest notion where he lived. Where would I look? No idea. I spent most of the afternoon riding around the church hoping he would appear. No luck. I did not see a soul. Finally I had to return home to help with the chores. When I arrived my uncle informed me that Tim had come out to the farm looking for me. Seeing me sitting next to my aunt, Tim knew where I lived. He showed more smarts than I did.

Well, it began. He was the friend I had been wanting all of my life. We hit it off. We both liked music. We had other common interests, but most of all we just enjoyed being with each other and when together we talked and talked. Having a friend to talk with was out of this world. One evening up in the hay mound our talking soon came to an end. We began to get more physical, which led to some tickling, which both of us enjoyed. Our hands began to wonder down to other places that were not only ticklish, but very exciting. Finally they reached that most private of all places on a man's body. It was very pleasurable. It was electrifying! "Hold it!" Cautioned my mind, "is this what friends do? I don't think so, but I sure like it." Since he was enjoying it as well, I continued exploring his body. After a while we stopped because Tim said he did not want to have an orgasm, whatever that was. We agreed that when we were playing around we would stop before either of us had an orgasm.

I knew the rest of the world, and in particular our parents, would not approve of what we were doing. But deep within me, I knew it was right, even if the rest of the world did not think so. This experience, of my inner being telling me something I was doing was right even if the rest of the world did not think so, would happen on more than one occasion. We did not get together just for sex. Our sexual encounters were not the most important aspect of our developing friendship. It was the close intimate relationship that counted. It was the joy of seeing Tim and spending time with him. The more moments together the better. Life had taken on a whole new meaning. Tim was someone who cared about me and I about him.

We both played the piano but Tim also played the organ. We began to work on a duet we would play as a prelude some Sunday morning. We both sang in the church choir. Tim lived in town and when I visited him we would get in his rowboat and paddle around the canal that ran through town. What I remember most about being with him was the enjoyment of just talking. It was a good friendship. It filled our needs at that time in our young lives.

One evening toward the end of summer our tickling had proceeded to caressing, then to feeling, and as the intensity gained in strength the moment to stop had arrived, but I let him continue and I experienced my first orgasm. I remember very little about the physical aspect of the experience. What I remember was the guilt I felt because I had broken our agreement. I did not feel guilty about the physical orgasm. From my perspective having the orgasm was really okay. Instinctively I felt we had been moving in that direction all summer and my having an orgasm was the natural consequence of the fondling we had been doing. But Tim seemed to be upset by what had happened. We did not say anything, and our evening ended shortly after that.

We continued to get together the rest of the summer, but we were more restrained. The spontaneity had left. We were not as comfortable with each other as we had been. We kept a respectable distance from each other. No tickling, no touching. We should have talked about what had happened, but no words came. I would return to my home in a few weeks, so we just stumbled along.

When I arrived home I began enjoying myself sexually. With that enjoyment came guilt. More guilt than I thought anyone could have. My upbringing had impressed on me that sex was only to be experienced within the confines of marriage and I was not married to myself. My sexual drive was very great, and I found myself caught between the pleasure of the act and the guilt which came with it. I did not give up sex. I endured the guilt. I began to blame Tim for my sexual activity. My Christian training had not taught me to take responsibility for my actions. I did not have the right to put the blame on Tim, even if that was a way out for me.

A few months after my return home, my uncle came to visit. When the front door opened, there was Tim with a great big smile on his face. I panicked. I did not want to see him. Too much guilt. I did not handle his visit with any grace or finesse. As far as I was concerned, he was the cause of my enjoying myself sexually and all of the guilt that went with it, and there he was smiling as if nothing had ever happened between us.

All I can say is that I treated him very badly. My response to his visit must have been very painful to him. End of friendship. I have not regretted our friendship or the sexual experience, but I have felt sad about how I ended it. Underneath my reaction was a lot of self-righteousness. I never saw him again. I think I asked about him a couple of times, but I never made any effort to see him. He has been in my memory ever since. Tim was an important part of my life. As I write about him there is a lump in my throat.

All of us have to come to terms with our sexuality and my experience with Tim was the beginning of mine. It was not and is not an easy task for any of us. One reason behind this is that we must die to being a child and come alive as an adult. This does not happen over night. It takes several years; and some people never seem to leave their childhood and become adults. The major thrust at this time is the maturing of our sexuality, located primarily in our sexual organs. The impact of this maturation is not only physical, but mental and spiritual. This is not an easy time in anyone's life. Many straight people, even with all the support systems within our culture, have a difficult time. For most gay people it is an extremely hard time and many do not make it because we get mixed sexual signals which are very confusing.

I remember my sexual struggles as well as my spiritual ones. They were interwoven throughout my life. Sexuality was not the common subject at the dinner table. Yet, in my life, sex made itself known mostly with men and not with women. As I became aware of my sexuality I talked with many gay men my age, and all ages, to know that coming to terms with being gay is a difficult task. I have met men who knew from the moment they were aware of sex, it was for persons of the same sex. But most gay men, including myself, grow up thinking we are straight, and low and behold we find that deep within us is a strange and wonderful attraction for persons of the same sex. That passion does not let go. What do we do with it?

For me this started with my friendship with Tim. I do not think I ever heard the word homosexual as a young person. I remember a couple of conversations between some of the guys at high school accusing someone they knew being a "queer." Even though they were not talking about me, inwardly, I knew they were. Their conversation indicated that a "queer" was the most despicable kind of person a young man could be. Throughout my junior and senior high school years I thought I had been looking for a close personal friend. But hindsight has revealed that I was really looking for a lover. Most people at this time in their lives have a close friend. This friendship is often their first love affair, but since it is usually with the same sex, sexual relations generally are not a part of the friendship. If sex does take place, it often ends the relationship.

My family was quite religious. We all went to Sunday school, church, youth program, sang in the choir. You name it, we did it. I did not feel I was forced into doing all of those activities. I simply did not question any of this. I enjoyed all of them.

Drinking, smoking, and certainly sex with women were all "No, No's." I was proud and quite self righteous. I knew I was better than anyone else simply because I was so religious. To me all situations in life were black or white. There were no areas of gray, and what I thought and felt was right. It was others who were wrong. There was no in-between. Put me on display. I am what you want. The perfect religious person.

The Second World War had begun during my senior year in high school and we were urged to go to college until we would be drafted. I received a scholarship to study agricultural at River Falls State Teachers College. In the Fall semester I took a course in animal husbandry, which was primarily a course on milk cows. The second or third meeting of the class was held in the barns where we were to judge three cows. They looked alike to me. They all had the proper appendages. The other students had several years of agriculture in high school and had judged cows before. This was my first try and I felt I was at a real disadvantage. I decided teaching agriculture was not for me and dropped my major. Nothing caught my interest and with no direction to the courses I took, I felt I was adrift.

One Saturday afternoon I went bowling. The alleys were in a tavern. When I walked in I noticed children having to spend their afternoon in that smoky place while their parents got drunk. Inwardly something said, "You need to do something about such a situation. Children should not be subjected to that." This happened for several weeks in a row before I decided God was calling me to the ministry. In the Presbyterian system a person does not decide to become a minister. God chooses you, calls you to the ministry just as God had called the great men in the Old Testament and Jesus had called his disciples. A person is called to the ministry by God, and this was my call. The decision made, I knew what I wanted to do.

About this time I decided I did not want to wait be drafted so I enlisted in the Army Air Force. Before the end of my first year in college, I was called into active duty. I flunked out as a fighter pilot and spent most of my time as a chaplain's assistant. Most of the chaplains I met did not measure up to my standard of religiosity. If those chaplains were good examples of ministers, I began to wonder about "the call" I had received. Maybe I had made a mistake. Maybe it had been my imagination, and God had not called me after all. I decided I would not become a minister. While in the service my religiosity did not stop me from having a few fleeting sexual experiences with men. If I had been caught I would have been sent home with a dishonorable discharge. I would have had to face my family. It would have been devastating.

After the war I returned to college. That summer I worked as a bellboy in a summer resort. Most of the clients came from Chicago to escape the heat and enjoy the out-of-doors. I was bothered by how hard those people worked at having a good time. Around four-thirty every afternoon the guests would return to the hotel from the afternoon's activity and go to their rooms. A little later they would reappear dressed to the hilt for the evening dinner followed by a night of drinking, playing cards, a popular board game, and some gambling. Life seemed to be one big party.

Watching this lifestyle bothered me. Once again that strange feeling deep within me seemed to be saying life was more than one big party and the answer would not be found in the world, but in the church. Once again 'the call' had come. I knew that I must enter the ministry. From that time on, I never doubted 'my call.' Since I was attending 'Cow College' as we lovingly called it, I decided to transfer to the University of Dubuque. There I could finish college and attend seminary.

Enter the second man in my life. I met Brad through a common friend. There he was. We became friends. His eyes, a shy smile, and a quietness about him began to capture me. After a while when we were together, I began to have the same feelings I had felt with Tim. I found myself catching a soft ball, just to be with him. I hated playing catch even with a soft ball. As far as I was concerned there was nothing soft about a soft ball. I could not catch a fly to save my life. Playing the infield or being a catcher was simply out of the question. But there I was, catching soft balls coming at me, who knows how fast. Brad loved softball. He wanted to be a pitcher and needed to practice, so I would go out with him and catch those cursed fast balls. I gritted my teeth, tried not to flinch and to hang on to as many of them as I could. Apparently I did all right because we practiced as often as our schedules allowed. After all, this was what all red-blooded men like to do. I would not let him know I really hated every minute of catching those balls. Recalling this, I guess unconsciously, I would have done anything just to be with him.

We both sang in the a cappella choir. I was president, and when it came time for Spring tour it was my job to decide who would be roommates. Of course I arranged for the two of us to be together. Great! No! Great mistake! There I was that very night in bed with him. His physical presence aroused physical, emotional, and sexual urges I could not ignore. Yet, I could not act on them either. I did not get much sleep. Keeping my hands where they belonged was next to impossible. On a couple of occasions they found their target for a very brief moment. I quickly took them away hoping my touch would not awaken him.

One night I thought he gave me a signal that he was interested sexually and I responded. But he continued to sleep and nothing happened. I was confused. Finally I turned over, but sleep refused to come. I did not have to lie there very long. It was soon time to get up because the choir had to leave around six in the morning. When we got up nothing was said and we joined the rest of the choir. We had three concerts, plus travel, making it a long day. In

3 1833 03003 2285

the final concert I did not sing the last group of songs. I was just too tired!

When we arrived at the home where we were to spend the night, I decided I needed to tell him what had happened the previous night, and what was going on with me. Guess what? It was the only time on tour we had twin beds. I went over to his bed, sat on the side, and with fear and trembling, poured out my heart to him. He did not get angry. He did not shove me away in disgust. He did not demand I find him another roommate for the rest of the tour. He did not turn away from me. He was not interested in having sex with me, or any man for that matter, but we would remain friends.

That was really too much. Here was a person who from all outward appearances was not a Christian. At least not like I was. Brad went to chapel services because they were required. His family did not say grace at meals, and their attendance at church was infrequent. Here I was, in a situation similar to that with Tim, but this time the tables were turned. I, the great Christian, was accepted by a person I had not considered to be a Christian, and our friendship was still intact. This so-called non-Christian had put my kind of Christianity to total shame. I have never forgotten that evening. The choir tour came to a close. We returned to school and there I was catching those cursed fast balls. The rest of the term went along as usual. At the end of the spring term, I graduated. We said good-bye and went our separate ways.

Despite my experiences with Brad and Tim and a few others sprinkled in between, I still felt I was like any other man. I had done some dating in the traditional sense while in college, but nothing serious. I simply was not in any hurry to find a girl and get married. I was sexually attracted to women, I thought. It was this sexual attraction for men that I did not understand. Even when I did date a woman, that attraction for men kept hanging around but

I never asked myself "Why?"

After two years at the University of Dubuque, I graduated, but decided not to attend the seminary. In fact the dean of the seminary suggested I go West. I packed up my bags and took off to the West Coast. I enrolled in the San Francisco Theological Seminary in San Anselmo, California. I had a few fleeting experiences with men, some in the seminary and some not. Looking back on all of this, I feel I simply did not want to accept this allure of men. I really did not want to think I was different. Since I had been attracted to men who were straight, then I was straight. I was sure I was the only man in this whole world who liked other men.

Toward the end of my first year in seminary I decided I was not getting any younger and I should consider getting married. I was directing a church choir and I began dating a woman who sang in the choir. One Saturday afternoon we were in San Rafael and went into a restaurant for a coke. When we walked in I saw my group of friends from the seminary sitting around a large table. We went over to them so I could introduce my fiancee to them. I began by introducing my friends to her. Around the table I went, giving the name of each of my friends. When I turned to introduce my fiancee, I drew a blank. I could not remember her name. My friends never let me forget that very embarrassing moment in time.

Looking back on that incident I now understand it was a subtle warning among others from my inner self saying, "Do not do this. Do not get married." I did not listen to any of the warning signs. Marriage came into the picture and I decided that before I went through with the marriage I ought to get some help with my problem. I went to one of the professors. He gave me a test to see if I was a homosexual. The test consisted of looking at pictures of men's faces. None of them were attractive. I flunked the test. His advice to me was that if after our marriage I could have sex with my wife that would take care of my interest in men. Fantastic! Maybe there was hope for me after all. The wedding was set for the end of August.

Following the spring term I went to the Northeastern part of Wisconsin. I was to serve as student pastor of four small churches. It would be a trial run to see if I really wanted to be a minister. The plan was for me to begin at 9:00 a.m. on Sunday morning. The first worship service would be fifty minutes in length, five minutes to shake hands, and ten minutes to drive ten miles, through the backwoods roads; repeating the whole process at the second church, and then on to the third. The third service would finish shortly after noon. The fourth service would be in the evening.

I had arrived on Saturday evening, met a few members of one of the churches and was then left on my own. I was not the epitome of assurance and self confidence. I decided to go to the church and practice the best sermon I had from my preaching class in seminary. It had about as much strength as a syrup-soaked pancake. So much for the "A" on that sermon. I went back to my room and went to sleep.

Fortunately, I only had two services to lead on that first Sunday. Although the sun was shining brightly there was not much sunshine in my heart as I set off for the first service. I arrived at a little crossroads of a town and quickly found the church. I tell you that church was small. I mean small. I walked in and stood up in the pulpit. There below me was a small group of men and women who had stone faces. Never before in my life, and not since, have I stood before a group of people whose faces were made of stone. They did not blink an eye. They did not cough. They did not move a muscle. I began the sermon with what little enthusiasm I had left, and just as I finished the last word, a man sitting in the back pew lifted his arms and let out a big yawn. End of service. Almost end of me. I shook hands as the people left and discovered they did not have stone faces. They thanked me for coming.

With ardor at less than half-mast I headed back to the town where I had spent the night. At least these people were alive. Upon arrival I greeted a few, went in and began the service. Not far from the church was the railroad, no problem, I thought. As I started the pastoral prayer a train did arrive, stopped and did some switching. It did not completely interrupt the prayer. It added some background noise to it. When it came time for the sermon, I stood up in the pulpit. As I was about to open my mouth up the center isle came a dog being chased by three small children. I managed to keep my composure and finished the service without any more interruptions.

The crowning blow came on Monday. I was asked to drive to a city, some sixty miles away, to visit some people who were in the hospital. On the way I wondered what I would say. Visiting hospital patients had not been in the curriculum. I do not remember what I said to them. What I have remembered was that every person I had visited died within two weeks. By the time I heard about those deaths, my life had settled down and I knew the ministry was for me. Before the end of the summer, the man who yawned so loudly that first Sunday was wearing his hearing aid and the people had shed their stone faces.

The middle of August arrived and it was time to return to California for my wedding. My mother and younger sister joined me as we drove from Wisconsin to California. The wedding was a gala affair. We were married in my wife's home church where I was the choir director. We went to Lake Tahoe for our honeymoon. I had no trouble having sex with my wife. All seemed to be going along as it should until the second day of our honeymoon. We went down to sun bathe on a dock. We had hardly started to enjoy the sun when I noticed two gorgeous men coming down to sun bathe. I could not keep my eyes or my mind off them. I took my wife's hand. That ought to help. No luck. There they were, and I could not stop sneaking glances at them. On came that bright light in the back of my mind. It was more like being hit on the head with a sledge hammer. The experts were wrong. I realized I would always be tantalized by the sight and presence of other men. I would forever be sexually attracted to them. The experts did not know what they were talking about. I would have to find an answer. Where did a person look for help when the experts were wrong?

I could function sexually with my wife, but I could not be intimate. Intimacy is the larger context in which sexuality takes place, and if it is not there, its absence changes the whole relationship. Physical intimacy – the holding of hands, looking into the eyes, the sheer enjoyment of each other's body – adds to the level of sex when it takes place. There is another level of intimacy which is even more important. It is emotional. This is the joy of being at one with the other person, of knowing their essence, of a deep emotional tie that binds you to them, filling your life to its fullness. Life is lifted up above just living and into a joyous adventure. When you look into the other person's eyes you go in and meet that person, the spirit, that dwells in that body. In this kind of intimacy sex becomes a total coming together of each person. I could function physically with my wife, but there was no intimacy. There was nothing either of us could do to change the situation.

Returning to the seminary to finish my senior year, I was glad my studies had destroyed my fundamentalistic approach to the Biblical material. A new and exciting way of finding the message of the Old and New Testaments had been offered and I had accepted it. The Historical-Critical method was giving me a method of Biblical study that made sense. It simply said that if we can know the time, the place, and the culture of any Biblical passage, we have a much better chance of understanding the text. When this happens, a person's insight to the meaning of the Christian faith becomes an exciting experience in the growth of the spirit. This is what I had been seeking.

I came under the influence of a small group of scholars known as Prophetic Realists. Simply put, they taught that Jesus interpreted his Messiahship in line with the teachings of the prophets of the Old Testament, as opposed to following the Jewish Apocalyptic thought patterns in the culture of the New Testament. The writers of Prophetic Realism felt Jesus fulfilled his Messiahship in terms of the Suffering Servant of the Lord as described in the Servant passages of Isaiah.

This is illustrated in the temptations. The real question put to Jesus was, "What kind of Messiah will you be?"

The Devil said, "Turn these stones into bread. Anyone who does that can be king."

Jesus replied, "No."

"Well," chided the Devil, "how about jumping off this cliff? God will not let you fall and kill yourself."

"Forget it," answered Jesus. "Performing miracles is not a valid foundation for religious faith." Finally the Devil took Jesus to the top of a mountain, and promised him all of the kingdoms of the world, if only he would bow down and worship him. Jesus replied, "Be off Satan! For Scripture says: "You must worship the Lord your God, and serve him alone." (1)

Those same temptations kept coming back to Jesus during his ministry. When he fed the multitude they wanted to make him king. Jesus walked away. Even when Jesus healed a person, he reminded them that it was their faith which had made them whole, not anything he had done. The end of his life and ministry was the cross and the Easter event. All of this was in line with the prophetic teaching in the Old Testament. He fulfilled his ministry as the Suffering Servant of the Lord, and not the Jewish Apocalyptic idea of a Messiah who would come from above with

16

a great army at his side.

Following seminary I became the pastor of a church in a small town in the middle of Wisconsin in the early 1950's. During that first year two other young couples joined the church, and we became friends. Great! Yes? No! One of the men stirred up all those sexual excitements within me. The old temptation was still there. It had risen once again. It had not gone away. Now what do I do? After coming close to succumbing to my desires, I did not yield, and I decided that any man who was involved in the life of any church I served as the pastor was off limits.

Shortly after we arrived our daughter was born. I always told people she came by train. The manse (the house provided by the church for the minister to use) was just across the street from the hospital and less than half a block was the mainline of the Milwaukee road. She was born just as the local passenger train arrived at the depot. So I told people they dropped her off.

A couple of years later our second child was on the way. One morning my wife said, "The baby is coming." I replied, "I don't have time for a baby today." I was only joking, but the day was full. We were in the midst of daily vacation Bible school, I had a funeral for the afternoon with the burial some fifty miles away. I arranged signals with the ladies of the church to use if the child arrived and I was still busy with Bible School. We did not use them. As I was about to have lunch the word came and I raced over to the hospital to see son and wife. They both were doing fine. She told me she had kept telling the doctor, "I have to have this child, I have to have this child," which he did not understand. Our son had arrived at noon. After a very short visit, I returned home and then to the funeral, the long ride to the cemetery and back. It was an eventful day, and when I arrived home my younger sister was there and helped us settle into a family life with a new child.

One day in Pastoral Psychology Magazine I saw an ad for the book *"The Homosexual in America"* It was the first book about homosexuality written by a homosexual following the Second World War. It did not take me long to send for that book. When it arrived, I kept it hidden in my desk. Reading it, a feeling of relief came over me. Now I knew what my attraction for men was all about and why it had not left as I had been told. I knew that with both Tim and Brad I had been looking for something more than a friend, a lover. More important, the book informed me I was not the only man who liked men on the face of this earth.

When I went out of town by myself I began to look for other gay men. I found them. Sometimes the encounter was good. At other times if sex was in the picture the accompanying guilt was so great I had to walk away. I was married and had children. That meant a commitment to the family. There were problems yet to be faced.

Understanding the basis of my interest in men, I wondered how I would feel if I saw Brad again. I decided we should visit him and his wife. We had a pleasant trip and it was great to see him again.

Following the evening meal, the two of us went for a walk. All the feelings I had had for him in college were still there, and to my surprise they were very strong. We returned to his house and joined our wives sitting next to them. I remember thinking, "He and I should be sitting together, alone." Then I understood the intensity of my feelings for him in our college years. I had been in love with him and had wanted to live with him. Impossible. He had not shared the same feelings for me. I was his friend. Nothing more. For years I had the fantasy of his calling me in the middle of the night asking me to come and live with him. I would have left everything and everyone and gone to him.

Psychiatry listed homosexuals as mentally ill. But I knew I was not mentally ill. I was no different from anyone else. If you cut me, I bled good red blood. My life was in order. I was successful in my vocation. In fact from the outside I was no different from any other man. The only difference between any other man and myself was that I was sexually attracted to men and fulfilled by them. The struggle continued, but at least I understood my situation, and in time I would find a satisfactory answer for my wife and myself.

If professional help was not available, or helpful, then what of my religious faith? I tried. I did all of the religious exercises a person was supposed to do to get help from God. I was in church every Sunday since the service depended on me. I read the scriptures. I prayed. And in those prayers I pleaded with God to take away this love of men, and replace it with the proper love for my wife. I made a few deals with God in my prayers. No answer. Nowhere in my seminary training, or in any of the theological books I had read, had anyone talked about how to handle the silences of God. I had been taught that if I pleaded enough, prayed enough, was persistent enough, I could force the God-up-there to do what I wanted. I made promises. I made a few bargains. There was no answer. No relief. This silence to my verdant pleas for help planted the seed of doubt about the God-up-there. Those sexually exciting men were out there. I would meet them and when they appeared I would be vulnerable. Deep within I knew I was living a lie. I would have to come to terms with that lie.

Inwardly I felt there had to be an answer somewhere. Could it be that the Biblical passages, which were used against gays like a sledge hammer, were being misinterpreted by the institutional church? The institutional church had been wrong before, and I hoped it was wrong in its idea of homosexuality. I would leave finding an answer to the scholars. As a pastor it was not my job to be a Biblical scholar. The pastor of a church does not have time to be a scholar, but does need to be able to read the scholars, find the kernel of truth in their writings, and translate it for the members in the congregation. For me the study of the Biblical material was never just an intellectual exercise. It was the pursuit of an understanding on how I as person, a Christian, was to live in this world and not just prepare myself for the next life. If the Bible did not really lead me into the fullness of my humanity, what good was it? I was sure someday scholars would discover that those passages used against homosexuals had been misinterpreted and the institutional church had been wrong once again. We gay people were not sick, nor monsters. We were persons. The only difference was our sexuality.

After my first pastorate I served in staff positions as the minister of Christian Education. For several years I attended the annual meeting of Christian Educators. Those meetings not only enabled me to get an excellent idea of what constituted good Christian Education, they also exposed me to new theological thinking being taught in some of the seminaries. These new theological ideas would become the foundation of my challenging the doctrine of God that would lead to "That Sunday."

One lecture which made a great impression was given by a well-known scientist who was a Christian. Here are the notes I took. "We live in a scientific and technological world. Even though the thought patterns and concepts of science keep changing, we change our thinking with them, and live by them. We live by the technical means which are the result of science. When we get sick we make use of the knowledge and skill of the doctors and the inevitable pills they subscribe. No one reckons with the direct intervention of some transcendent power. We do not really believe in 'so-called' miracles because they do not fit into the known ways we have observed the universe to function. If there is an event which is different from what we know, we do not rest until we have found a rational cause."

The professor was sixty when he gave those lectures. He said, "I have lived in three worlds. The first was the world of horse and buggy, the steam locomotive, coal and kerosene, and the ice refrigerator. The second was the world of the automobile, the diesel engine, the airplane, and electricity. The third was that of the atom and its nucleus, of space exploration and of automation. If around the 1900's a person lived at the rate of one world per life-time, by 1925 at the rate of two, and by 1950 at the rate of three, and our children are already living at the rate of four very different intellectual worlds per life-time, what will the future be?

"There was a time when the Western World was Christian in the sense that the basic concepts and symbols of the Christian faith were integral to the prevailing structure of thought. In principle at least we knew of these things, and some people lived by them and others did not. In either case people looked to the church for guidance in virtually all matters. When a plague struck, or a drought scorched the earth, or floods swept away their possessions, they assembled in church to plead with God in prayer.

"That age was gone. The existing knowledge we already have, to say nothing of that which is still to come, has undermined virtually all of this. To most modern people, the concepts of Scripture simply get in the way. Even the term 'God' is no longer a basic idea for our contemporary culture. For all practical purposes God is dead. People no longer pray for food, rain, health, or success. Nature is thought to be essentially independent of God, and we feel no need for God."

His words struck a note with some of the sneaking suspicions I had been harboring. His lectures convinced me that perhaps it was time for the church to come up with a new name for God. I kept thinking, "Is it heresy to suggest we need a new name for God? Do we ring our hands, cry tears of sorrow and shake our heads in disbelief and feel sorry for those who think this way?" Of course not. Such thinking should send us back to the scriptures with greater fervor and determination. With a sense of urgency and excitement we need to dig into the Old and New Testaments and find the meaning of the words of the writer. Never in the life of the institutional church has there been such an exciting time to witness to our belief that God was in Christ reconciling the world unto himself.

Another speaker at that conference added fuel to the fire. He spoke about new ways of thinking about God. He suggested that if our thinking about God was Biblically and theologically correct we did not need to change. But if it was not right, then we did need to change. He pointed out that our concept of God was built upon the model of the Caesars, Napoleon, Alexander-the-Great. We think in terms of a supreme God, a supreme spiritual power who lives above us, who created and sustains the universe and who with a snap of a finger caused the universe to be. Everything which happens in this world is under His/Her thumb. We have also been taught that this kind of "God" can be bribed to do our bidding if we are very religious.

As these ideas were fermenting within me, I was introduced to John A. T. Robinson's book *Honest to God.* His book raised and answered many of the questions about traditional Christianity which had been plaguing me. In his book I was introduced to the writing of Dietrich Bonhoeffer. One idea from Bonhoeffer stuck in my mind. He said that God was not a power machine who, when we got in deep trouble of our own making, could be called upon to pick us up, lift us out of our trouble and set us down somewhere else free. That figure of speech never left my mind. I continued to mull over some of his ideas and in time they would demand that I voice them. Their time was not yet.

At this time I was the Associate Pastor of Christian Education in a large church in the middle of Wisconsin. One day our daughter became sick and had to go to the hospital. My wife was quite upset because I was not as upset as she was by what had happened.

I did not see any reason to get excited because our daughter had to go to the hospital. I would wait until we heard from the doctors. If the news was not good, then I would begin to worry. It turned out our daughter did not have anything to cause us concern. For some reason (not clear to me at the time, but understood later) I decided to tell my wife that I was attracted to men. A few months later I had my first experience of being impotent with my wife.

I had met a man and we were seeing each other. He had come to terms with his sexuality. I was still struggling with mine. In his presence a long-held suspicion of mine was confirmed. Physical intimacy came naturally with him. Conversion flowed easily. I discovered I was whole, complete, and truly myself with him. It was a bittersweet situation. I would feel guilty when we were together. I was not being faithful to my wife. At the same time I did not want the moments together to end, and when we parted I looked forward to our next meeting. I was playing with fire. Someone was going to get burned. Fortunately I did not fall in love with him and the affair was short-lived.

As the Associate Minister of Christian Education of this Presbyterian Church with a very large membership in the middle of Wisconsin with many important people of the community as members, I was vulnerable for any indiscretion on my part. The indiscretion happened. I was a leader in Christian Education throughout the state and participated in many workshops which enabled me to travel throughout the state. When traveling I was on the lookout for other gay men. I discovered I was not good at finding them. Since I had lived most of my life in small towns, I was not ready for the big cities and cruising got me in trouble. I was rolled or robbed on more than one occasion.

I had been asked by the Children's Division of the National Council of Churches to be a leader in a workshop for teachers in Ohio.

Since I could not reach my destination in one day I spent the evening in Columbus. That evening I went cruising. It was not a good idea. I was too naive, too honest, too trusting of others to be out cruising. I was not the aggressor. But I was available, and if approached, I would respond in the affirmative. I was approached and I responded in the affirmative. He spent the night. I knew nothing about hustlers or their method of operation. I revealed too much information about myself to the man. Sexually he was a dud. In the morning he became very nasty and demanded that I pay him some money or he would expose me to the church I served and the town in which I lived.

I sent a quick, desperate prayer to the God-up-there to come to my aid, to lift me up and out of that terrible situation, set me down safely somewhere else, and wipe out the whole horrid mess. No such luck. Bonhoeffer was right. God did not function as a power machine, who would come to my rescue. I had created the situation, and I would have to find an answer. The man was a blackmailer who knew how and what to do. I do not remember much about the course of events, but I did everything he demanded to get rid of him. I promised to pay him some money and finally he left. I did get some money and had enough presence of mind to pay him through Western Union. I would have proof he had received it.

When I arrived at the workshop I was all smiles on the outside and a bundle of nerves ready to explode on the inside. Every time the door opened I was sure he would be there. After a long nerve-racking day and a night of little sleep, I had a chance to call home. My wife informed me the blackmailer had called at one a.m. that morning. All I remember of our conversation was her question as to whether or not I had functioned with him. I replied in the affirmative. She did not respond to my answer. She did say that the senior pastor of the church had been to the house at her request. "Good." I thought. He would give her the support, comfort, and help she needed for this crisis in our lives. I told her I would return immediately but was going to stop in Madison, Wisconsin to talk with a lawyer I knew from my days in the service.

Arriving in Madison my lawyer friend was not in his office. He was out of town. I had to take another chance and decided I would talk to his partner. He was sympathetic and told me that if the blackmailer called again I was to tell him I had contacted a lawyer and any further demands would have to be made through my lawyer. I was instructed to warn the blackmailer that if he bothered either my wife or me, my lawyer would call the FBI. Armed with these assurances, I continued my drive home. I wondered if my wife would be there. Had she taken the kids and left? If so, I could not blame her. I began to prepare myself for coming home to any empty house. The thought made me sick.

When I arrived home, she had not left. We talked about what had happened and finally went to bed. At one a.m. the phone rang. We figuratively jumped out of our skins. When I answered, it was the blackmailer. I told him what the lawyer had instructed me to tell him. That was the last we heard from him. That was not the last time we jumped to the high heavens when the phone rang late at night. We talked about our situation and made some decisions and plans for the future. I do not remember them all.

One decision was that I would seek the help of a psychiatrist. Another was to look for another church I could serve. The senior pastor agreed it was best for all concerned that I look for another church. In the midst of all this turmoil, my wife and I both developed an ulcer. We jokingly told people we could not stand each other which was partly true. I have had great difficulty writing these few paragraphs. My stomach has been tied up in knots. My fingers keep hitting the wrong keys.

That was a critical time in our lives. Many years later I learned that my wife had decided to stay with me because she would have help in raising the children. From the very beginning of our marriage, I had taken my share of the work with the children. I did all of the night feeding, changing of diapers, and getting up with them if needed. For a while my daughter woke up every night around two in the morning and I would read a comic book to her. And every night at a certain place in the story I would laugh. I smile now as I recall that story. She would go back to sleep. I would go back to sleep. At age five my son was an early riser. I would get up with him and often we went for a ride in the car giving the rest of the family a few more moments of sleep.

One summer when the children were still young, we were on our way to the West coast to visit my wife's family. We stopped to spend the night with a seminary friend who lived in Nebraska. That meant we were two hours ahead of them. The next morning our kids slept later than usual. They woke up at seven our time, but five o'clock Nebraska time. I took the kids, found a park and proceeded to pass the time. The town was still sleeping. Every now and then a delivery truck would pass, slow down and look at that crazy man with two children playing in the park at that time of the morning. I got the kids to laughing so hard my son wet his pants. End of visit to the park.

It was now seven a.m. Nebraska time. Returning to the house we found our host and hostess were still sleeping. All of this time my wife had been searching for something for the kids to eat. The cupboards were bare. We were about to go to a restaurant when we heard a stirring. Someone had finally gotten up. The cereal was under the sink, the one place my wife had not looked. As long as we were together as a family my wife would have my help in raising the children.

A second important result of my wife's decision to remain in the marriage was that I would go to a psychiatrist. I hoped he would "cure" me of this desire for men. No such luck. In fact he was no help period. After a few visits I decided I was not getting anywhere and I stopped seeing him. Meanwhile my wife and I had come to an arrangement that worked for both of us as well as possible under the circumstance. We did not fight. We supported each other in matters regarding the family. In every church we served, we would find one or two couples who became friends and formed the basis of a social group. The decision to stay together enabled me to continue to function in my profession. Without this I would have faced a divorce, and in the late fifties, I do not think I would have been able to continue in the ministry. Our life was not one dull moment after another, we did have many good times.

A third important result of the blackmail was the decision to look for another church. After much frustration, a call came from the chairman of the pastor-seeking committee in Coos Bay, Oregon. I had been highly recommended. I flew to Coos Bay, met with the committee. They liked me. I liked Coos Bay. With hearts and spirits somewhat higher than they had been, we packed up and took off to Oregon. We were back on the West Coast. Fine. I had wanted to return to the West Coast for a long time.

Soon after we were settled, we decided to try another psychiatrist. This time we went together, but he did not see us together. He started with me. I told him the problem and to my surprise he said that it would take him about three months to handle it. The essence of what I received from him in that first session was that if I was gay I should be gay and stop fooling around with it. That took care of that. Not quite. It was easier said than done. He also pointed out to me that the reason I had told my wife of my interest in men, when our daughter had been sick, was I had unconsciously decided to get out of the marriage. That decision also had something to do with the fact I was having difficulty performing sexually with my wife. That was the first sane advice I had

27

received. Finally an authority figure had told me being gay was okay. I could look at men without feeling guilty. I did not have to deny those feelings. I began to feel good about myself.

My wife's turn was next. She did not spend as much time with him as I had. We left, got in our car and returned to Coos Bay. On the way she informed me that he had told her to get out of the marriage. We talked about what he had told us and decided to remain married. We could stay together for the sake of our children. We could give them two parents who loved them. We had never fought each other through our children. That had always been a "No-No." Any disagreements were settled without the children being present. We would continue that policy. In the meantime the emotional and sexual needs we had which could not be fulfilled by the other we would handle ourselves.

In moving to Coos Bay we were closer to my wife's family, but visits were limited primarily to summer vacations. We felt it would be good for our children to have foster grandparents. Two families in the congregation began to fulfill this need. They performed all of the duties of grandparents. They attended various school functions, exchanged presents at Christmas and birthdays and performed other grandparent functions. We did not use them for baby sitting. When the children had a special time, they often asked their foster grandparents to be with them. To this day they still have that special relationship.

Robert R. and his family also played an important part in the life of our family. His two older children were about the same age as ours. The two families often spent holidays together. Robert R.'s family and the foster grandparents formed the basis of our social life. Picnics in the summer time, holidays, and other special social events were spent together. This group formed an extended family, and for all practical purposes we were a normal family. No one knew the secret we had to live with. In Coos Bay we began a new life, and I began a new ministry.

A cool breeze came through the window of the car and stopped the memories which had been going through my mind. It was a nice relief from the heat. The cool breeze meant I was nearing the coast. I had gotten through the heat of the day without having to resort to the air conditioner. Good. Soon I would see the Pacific Ocean and enjoy the rest of the trip to Coos Bay. It felt good to drive down the coast highway with its hills, sand dunes, and special vegetation. In a short time I would be in Coos Bay, the place where my spiritual, sexual, and personal journey would be lived out to its proper conclusion.

THE JOURNEY BEGINS

THAT SUNDAY

This was my first visit to Coos Bay since I had resigned as pastor. I would be meeting with members who were still alive and had been part of the spiritual journey from its beginning to its end. In my Christmas letter the previous year, I had asked them to write to me about their experience in the Coos Bay church. Since none of them were writers they had asked me to meet with them. In a group they would be able to share what the journey had meant to them. Before going to the home of my host, I stopped at the church, went in, sat down in a pew and was struck by how much the physical building itself had been affected by my ministry. I wondered how much it had affected the lives of the members.

Closing my eyes, I remembered the day my family and I drove into that same parking lot on our arrival in Coos Bay. The building we saw did not look much like a church. My children thought it looked more like a motel. But the sign in front of the building informed us it was the First Presbyterian Church of Coos Bay. So we knew we were in the right place.

We got out of our car and went up to the front door. It was unlocked. We went in and found ourselves in a small entryway that led to the back of the sanctuary. The fellowship hall was on our immediate right. The sanctuary on the left. It was simple, and the simplicity gave me the feeling I might hear "the still small voice of God," and I felt this would be a good sanctuary in which to preach. The year was 1963 and my ministry would emphasize preaching and teaching. As far as we know, Jesus did not start a Sunday school, develop an outstanding youth program, have multiple choirs, or construct a magnificent building for all such activities. He was not worried about the future. He challenged people to the importance of the present. He gathered a small

31

group of adults and shared with them his teachings and his life. I would try to follow that example.

In 1963 Coos Bay was the world's largest lumber-shipping port. This meant a town with longshoremen, lumber jacks, truck drivers, and a reputation as a very red-neck city. This was impressed on us the day we arrived in Coos Bay. After we had left the church, looked around the town, we went to a pizza parlor and sat next to a window near the entrance. While waiting for our pizza a car drove up, stopped and two young men got out. I noticed another man sitting in the back of the car. He sat up, pushed the front seat forward, opened the door. He was kneeling down facing the front door of the pizza parlor and began to urinate. I did not quite believe what I saw. I looked at my wife, "Do you see what I see?" "Yes." We sat there, not quite believing what we saw. As the man continued to urinate others in the parlor had noticed and came over to the windows to watch. The two young men who had come in to order a pizza suddenly realized what was happening and tried to disassociate themselves from the one in the car. No way. They hung their heads in shame. Finally their friend stopped, fell back into his seat and gave a big sigh of relief. Welcome to Coos Bay! We stayed some fourteen years.

As I began to write this book I asked my son-in-law what he thought about Coos Bay when he had arrived. He replied, "A town of white men, in trucks, with guns." He had come from a large city in the East were only the bad guys displayed guns in their vehicles. Counter to this rather macho image, there were a number of talented people in the various fields of art, a good community theater and a community college which featured adult education and the first two years of college studies. The business district of Coos Bay was located on the West side of the Coos River. One wonderful memory of Coos Bay was to be driving on the north-bound street and there on my right, hardly an arm's length away, towering high above me, would be a large ocean-going vessel with logs stacked high on the deck. I always felt a bit small alongside such a huge ship. It was an experience I always enjoyed.

Preaching was (and still is) important in the Presbyterian church. It is not the all-wise minister standing up before his congregation and sprinkling his great words of wisdom over infertile heads. Preaching comes out of the minister's struggle with the Biblical message and applying it to the world in which we live. That kind of preaching is seldom a message of comfort. The members of the Coos Bay church were no different from those in any other church and I did not feel they needed a message of comfort. They needed to be confronted with the offense of the Gospel. It was this mysterious offense that promised to bring wholeness and completeness to a person's life.

The Bible is more than just a bunch of pious platitudes for use on Sunday morning in a worship service and then left there until the next week. The Bible contains the way to the fullness of our humanness; but it also says there is a cost. I was well aware that the motivation in the life of Jesus was the Suffering Servant of the Lord. I also knew deep within, whether a person liked it or not, that was the only way. The good news of the Gospel is the promise of the fullness of life, if a person is willing to pay the price. If not, then be prepared for much sorrow, unhappiness, and pain.

For me, preaching took a great deal of time and mental gymnastics. Almost as soon as I left the church on a Sunday morning, next week's sermon invaded my mind and was constantly making itself known. Monday and Tuesday were spent in reading and research of the scripture passage I would use as the basis of the sermon. Wednesday I began to write the sermon that was to be finished by noon on Friday. This process helped me clarify my thinking and kept the length of the sermon to about twenty minutes. I did not sit at my desk and think. Thinking was done on my feet and often I would just walk to help clarify my thinking. Driving to a meeting

33

gave me an abundance of time to think about the sermon for the coming Sunday. I also have a mind that is never still. Something is always going on and even in sleep, my mind is filled with dreams.

For a long time I had been bothered by the doctrine of the God-up-there. From the desperate plea to the God-up-there to remove my homosexuality, the disturbing ideas at continuing education conference, plus the theology of Bishop Robinson and Dietrich Bonhoeffer concerning the doctrine of God, had captured my mind and would not let go. One day walking back to the church, following a coffee break, I said to myself, "Okay Hannon, it's high time you come clean with your congregation. Stop stalling. They need to know that you do not believe in the God-up-there. No matter what may happen, this coming Sunday is the day you must begin to preach about the doctrine of God."

Sunday arrived. It was January 16, 1966. Sitting in the pews were some professional people, business men and women, teachers from all levels of education, a sprinkling of laborers, and a few people who were on the fringes of the economic world. My two children sat in the second row from the front on my left as they had done every Sunday since our arrival. On my right were three little old ladies who also had been there every Sunday. The members of the congregation had been used to hearing the usual quasi-fundamentalism given in most Protestant churches. The familiar message of comfort, certainly nothing that would jar the status quo or challenge the mind. Since my arrival I had suggested the message of the Gospel came with a demand. That I would say something different on a Sunday morning was not new, but I do not think that they were ready for what I was about to say.

"That Sunday" started like any other Sunday Morning. We followed the order of service as usual. When it came time for the sermon, I stood up and said, "All that I have been taught and all that I have taught and preached for the past fifteen years in the

34

ministry, I feel that I have been sold a bill of goods and I do not believe any of it. We will begin a spiritual trek in the wilderness. I hope it does not take us forty years to find some answers as it did Israel in the Old Testament." That caught their attention. I continued, "What I am going to say comes from my struggle over a long period of time with the doctrine of God.

"There are several ideas about God that we must discard. Many people have little to do with God until life comes tumbling in and then they call on God for help. Two young people, just out of high school were married. She had been raised in the Christian tradition. He had seldom darkened the door of any church. After the wedding they took off to the East coast where he served in the navy on a submarine. On his first trip out to sea his buddies warned him that when they returned his wife would not be waiting for him with the other wives. When they docked, she was not there. She had returned to her family

"He got an emergency leave and came looking for her. When he arrived she would have nothing to do with him. He went to the minister who had performed the marriage and related what had happened. He concluded by saying that even though he did not attend church he did believe in God, and while at sea he had prayed and pleaded with God that she would be waiting for him. His pleas were not answered. Asking God for help when all else has failed simply does not work.

"Many people have been taught that God is their conscience. While there is a vague, religious, Christian tradition in our culture, our consciences develop more from our breeding than religion. Take, for instance, someone who enjoys hunting and has been trained from their youth that shooting a sitting bird is a 'No, No.' Should they accidentally kill a sitting bird they would suffer pangs of guilt. But shooting a bird on the wing twenty yards away is okay. That is sport. That person's conscience is the result of his family and society's training, not of God.

"Another idea which has persisted throughout the ages is that God is an old man with a long beard who lives up-there somewhere. In a church school class the children were asked what they thought about God. Most of the children answered, 'God is a very old gentleman living in heaven.' Their response was natural because to most children, their parents and other adults are 'old,' and God most be the oldest of all. Unfortunately many children do not overcome this idea and often carry it into their adult life.

"These ideas persist because many of us have been taught to take the Bible literally. The pages of the Old Testament are filled with anthropomorphisms, a big word, which means the writers talk about the hands, the heart, the blood, the bowels of God. They did this because of the difficulty of the Hebrew language to express religious ideas. Different parts of the body were used to express religious and emotional ideas. The writers were not concerned about the physical aspects of God. They were concerned about the response of Israel to the saving events of God. The primary historical event in the Old Testament was the Exodus, and the rest of the Old Testament is a commentary on Israel's response and understanding to that event. The writers also thought of God as He. In their time that was all they could do. The use of the pronoun 'he' to refer to God has lead most of us to think of God as a person. It is this concept which must die. Easier said than done.

problem. We encounter the world view of Jewish apocalyptic thinking. In this understanding the world had been created by God, but was ruled by the Devil, or Satan, and his army of demons. The evil spirits of this world were the cause of all wickedness, sin and disease. Against this powerful kingdom stood God with his army of angels.

Heaven was above, hell below, and earth in the middle. The forces of these two worlds were locked in mortal combat. Fine. Except they fought their battles in the lives of the people on earth. Not fine. For instance, if a person was sick, it was because they were possessed by a demon, and only an angel or some other person from above could exorcise the evil spirit out.

"We do not live in a three-story universe. We live in a scientific, technological world. We depend on the knowledge of the scientific world to solve our problems. When we get sick, we make use of the skills of the doctor plus the inevitable pills they subscribe to make us well. Very few people believe in the direct intervention of some transcendent power. If there is an event which is different from what we know, science does not rest until it has found a rational cause. From the scientific point of view God does not exist. Nature is essentially independent of God and many people do not really feel any need for God.

"In traditional Western Christianity people are taught that God is Almighty, All-powerful, All knowing. This idea has led many people to think of God as a Being who can be bribed to do our bidding. If a person prays enough, attends worship every Sunday, does other prescribed religious activities, they can get the God-up-there to fulfill their request. The difficulty of this understanding is that we have been assured that when we have gotten ourselves in a real mess, with no way out, we can turn to the God-up-there for help. But what happens if the God-up-there does not come to our aid?

"There was a young college student who had not spent much time in study or attending classes. His father died just before semester exams. A friend asked him if this would affect him. The young man shook is head saying, 'No, I am sure God will see me through. Now that dad is gone and mother is depending on me, I am trusting in God' He

37

flunked! The identification of the Christian faith with a transcendent God is not vital to the message of either the Old or New Testament.

"Besides our preaching and teaching, the idea of a God-up-there is reinforced by the very shape of our churches. Most of them have high walls, stained glass windows, tall ceilings and roofs crowned with spires pointing to the God-up-there. Within the walls of the church is the sanctuary, the most sacred of all places, which has been set aside from the rest of the building, and dedicated to the religious realm – God's realm – and not to the world outside.

"Within these sacred walls people come to worship. A mother took her young son to church. He was greatly impressed by the music of the choir and the organ. When the usher came marching down the aisle to take the offering, he was sure they were God's soldiers. When they had finished, the lights in the sanctuary were turned down low and quietness descended. The minister stood up, ascended to the pulpit, and a spotlight came on bathing him in light. At that moment the boy turned to his mother and asked, 'Is it commercial time?' It was more, it was brain washing time. Worship is the most important religious activity most Christians do. All that takes place is an offering to the God-up-there which leaves the impression that worship is concerned with what is 'holy' rather than common; what is 'religious' and not 'life.'

"Worship is meant to prepare us for action in the world. We might liken worship to a football team between halves. The coach makes the necessary changes in the game plan to enable the team win. So with worship. All that takes place should prepare us to go out into the world as the 'saving ones' not the 'saved ones,' living God's life in the midst of the world. It is the world God loves, and worship should prepare us to be involved in the world.

"Much of worship is some form of prayer. There is the

prayer of confession of sins, the pastoral prayer which is really a chance for the minister to tell the God-up-there what is wrong with this world, often a prayer of thanksgiving, and a few other types of prayer sprinkled in. All of these prayers are addressed to the God-up-there in the hope that we have done our religious best. Most of us have been taught that it is necessary for us to pray and the more we pray the better off we will be. But I question this. A minister was once asked, 'How many hours do you spend on your knees each day in prayer? He replied, 'I do not spend as much time as you think is necessary, but I go up and down the streets of this crowded city and hundreds of people, young and old, weary and forlorn pass me. I look into their faces and pray for them. Not on my knees, but on my feet I spend time in prayer.'

"Another idea which we need to discard is that an object, or a place, is holy and has special powers. Having sacred objects or places appeals to many people. It gives them a shortcut to being religious when ordinary methods have failed. The idea of a 'holy place' reached its worse understanding at the time of the Crusade. A great cry was sounded throughout Christendom to save the birthplace of Jesus from the heathens. The number of people killed in the name of the Prince of Peace seeking to save his birthplace is unbelievable. It is not by accident that we do not know where Jesus was born, or where the cross stood, or where he was buried. It was to prevent anyone from making those places holy, endowing them with special powers, and that is exactly what the institutional church has done.

"Closely related to religious places and objects is the idea of 'saints.' They are persons whose spirituality has evolved way above the rest of us. No way! In the New Testament we find twelve unlettered men and a scattering of women, none with a college degree or political pull, who formed the foundation of the early church. In the first hundred years of

39

the church's life the 'saints' were primarily slaves and lower class people. They shared and lived a new life found within the community of believers. They did feel they had been separated out of this world by God, yet they were in the midst of their world, witnessing in the market place, in the homes of their masters, and sometime in front of lions and gladiators.

"The final sacred concept we need to attack are the so-called miracles. The people who lived during the time of the Bible were stirred with a sense of awe and wonder of their natural world. They knew and understood the basic rhythm of nature and when something unusual happened they did not call it a 'miracle.' It was a sign. It probably had some hidden meaning, but was not seen as the setting aside of the laws of nature.

"The healings of Jesus are also interpreted as being miraculous. In the Gospel of Matthew there is an account of a man who, possessed by an evil spirit, was brought to Jesus, and Jesus healed him. The healing was not a matter of Jesus setting aside the laws of nature, it was a battle between Satan and Jesus. Because Jesus had cured the man, the bystanders were amazed and wondered who Jesus was. The response of the Pharisees was, 'It is only by Beelzebub, prince of devils, that this man drives the devils out.' Jesus responded, 'Every kingdom divided against itself goes to ruin; and no town, no household, that is divided against itself can stand. And if it is Satan who casts out Satan, Satan is divided against himself; how then can his kingdom stand?' (1)

"In almost all of the healings in the Gospels Jesus pointed out that it was the person's faith in him which produced the healing. Jesus refused to do the miraculous at the time of his temptation and later in his ministry he reminded those who came to be healed that it was their faith which had healed them. In Jesus we see the man totally for others and totally for God. A man among human beings so attuned to what God intended for human beings that those who knew him were convinced he was the Christ, in whom God's love was at work."

Our journey had begun. Many of the traditional and sacred ideas of institutional Christianity had be raised and found wanting. I was on the right track. I was not alone. The No-God theologians of the sixties were coming into their own and I quoted them to indicate to the people in the congregation I was not the only person questioning these time-honored and sacred ideas of the doctrine of God. If the Christian faith was to have any relevance in this world, it would need to restate the doctrine of God.

A BRAVE BEGINNING

The attack which started on "That Sunday" had reached its conclusion. All that was sacred to Presbyterians and most mainline churches had been challenged and much had been discarded. From the theological side little was left to tear down, our bridges had been burned, there was no going back. I wondered what the members thought. While I had been giving the sermons I watched for telltale signs of their reactions. Coughs, clearing of throats, fidgeting are signals to anyone speaking that the audience is not with them. I had watched for such signs, but they were not there. I had noticed the members had been attentive. They had been listening.

It was customary for the minister to stand at the entrance of the church as the members left. I watched for any indication of how they felt. If they said, "That was a wonderful sermon," I knew they were either lying or had not heard a word I had said. If they smiled and said nothing I knew they had heard and had been disturbed. Good. Something positive was happening. They had not gotten up and walked out. They had not turned me over to the Presbytery and asked for a heresy trial. They had not yawned, settled back in their pews and appeased that little bald headed man up there who had really taken off on a tangent this time.

Literally they had clapped their hands and shouted for joy. During the coffee hours which followed those sermons, many expressed their thanks and confessed they had entertained some of the same ideas. A few people on the streets of Coos Bay stopped me and said, "I have heard what you have been preaching. That's great. Keep up the good work." I was somewhat puzzled by their response and finally decided they felt good because a minister had the courage to voice their questions and doubts from the pulpit.

Those sermons were given over a period of six months and somewhere in the middle I was invited to a luncheon meeting. Upon arriving someone said to me, "You know, I am convinced more and more that the church will just have to change if it is going to get across to the world what it represents and what its message is." I replied, "Well, you should have been in our church, because I got rid of God, and now all of our problems are solved."

We chuckled about that remark, but the man was concerned that the message of the church which was important to him and to others was not being heard. Later during lunch the person sitting across the table from me, with no prodding on my part, expressed the same idea. Our journey had begun. I was on the right track and going in the right direction. I strongly felt the time had come for all of Christendom to call a huge council to reconsider and reformulate the doctrine of God.

From a practical point of view it was July and in Coos Bay, as in all of Oregon, the summer slump in attendance had taken place. What had been said since "That Sunday" had been intense. The emotional strain of tearing down the central theological concept of

God had taken its toll on me. I needed time for reflection. Had I gone in the right direction popped into my mind on more then one occasion. Had I received a telegram instructing me to the top of a mountain where I would receive a new book filled with answers would have helped. No way. It would have negated all I had said.

When I first arrived in Coos Bay I was scrounging around in the secretary's office and found a set of the original plans for the building. If they had been completed the Coos Bay Presbyterian church would have been a nice standard church with high pointed ceiling and spire. I asked someone what had happened and they told me that after the building had been started they had run out of funds and were not able to finish the building as designed. A contractor offered to finish the building with the available funds. He cut off the high ceiling, put on a flat roof, giving the structure a slightly compressed look. No wonder my children thought the church looked like a motel. They had been used to a massive, impressive building, covering half a city block; a tribute to the God-up-there, not this chopped-off edifice in Coos Bay. Having attacked the idea of a God-up-there, we discovered we did not need a building with a high pointed ceiling with spire pointing to the God-up-there.

It was the sanctuary which needed some help. As you sat in a pew you looked at a round stained glass window which would have fit very nicely in a wall with a high ceiling. Instead you had a round window in a compressed wall. It did not fit. Below the window the choir sat facing the congregation. Below them was the communion table, and the pulpit was on the left side of the congregation. The Session asked Robert R. to design a new format for the chancel. He decided to remove the stained glass window and place it in the entry way. The advantage of this change was that its colors bathed you when you entered and left. We did not get as much flack over that as I had expected. In its place Robert R. designed a long narrow cross which became the center of a person's attention.   The chancel was divided with the choir on both sides, the communion table in the middle and the pulpit on the right side.

Robert R. was an architect and elder in the church.   He was a pillar in the congregation. He was the perfect church leader from my point of view. He was respected in the community. His views on any subject matter were sought and followed. He was a quiet person with a subtle sense of humor.   He had learned that we only tease someone we like. He and I got along very well. He had one great passion. Sailing. On the weekends he spent as much time as possible in his sail boat.   He was not tied to the past either theologically or in social matters. Most important of all – from the standpoint of a minister – Robert R did not have an agenda of his own that so often happens with persons who are "pillars" in the local church. Since he was part owner of his business he was free to attend meetings of Presbytery as the delegate from the Coos Bay church. He was a strong foundation of support throughout all the challenges and changes the congregation would confront.

Since many people were gone on weekends during the summer to who knows where, certainly not to church, I suggested our worship service be held on Wednesday evening. The Session members thought that was too much of a change and finally decided we would have two services during the summer months. The primary service would be held on Wednesday evening and repeated the following Sunday. This would give the people a choice of time, Wednesday evening or the traditional Sunday morning. In June the attendance at the two services was about equal, but beginning in July more people attended Wednesday evening than Sunday morning. The total number of people for both services was greater than the previous summer with only a Sunday service.

Included in the remodeling of the chancel was the installation of a new pipe organ. After three years of putting up with an electronic instrument I had persuaded the Session and members of the congregation we should have a pipe organ. The fact I also play the pipe organ may have had something to do with it. At that time electronic organs were not worth the money. The music in a worship service is more important than many people realize. I was well aware of the power of hymns in teaching theology. I always had the sneaking suspicion more theology was taught through the hymns than all the sermons put together. Whether the people sang them or not, they heard the music and unconsciously repeated the words reinforcing their beliefs through the power of the music. I felt we should have the best instrument available – the pipe organ.

The remodeling of the chancel had been timed to coincide with the arrival of the pipe organ. I had told Robert R. the organ chamber needed as hard a plaster finish as possible. This would enable the sounds to mingle and then come out in the fullness and richness which the organ would have. The chancel walls were also finished with hard plaster and hard woods. This made our choir of ten to twelve people sound like one of fifty or sixty voices, and indeed it did.

The pipe organ arrived in a large truck. Soon the isles of the sanctuary were filled with boxes of all sizes and shapes. In a short time they were unpacked and pipes of all sizes and shapes were exposed. The tallest pipes were eight feet in length but the organ chamber was not tall enough to accommodate them and the wind chest they sat in. No problem. The company had bent the tops so they would fit. The shape of pipe does not affect the sound. It is determined by length, width and the composition of the materials used in making the pipe. The smallest pipes were only a few inches in length. When put together they produce that marvelous, majestic sound which is the trademark of pipe organs. Most of installation time spent was connecting the electrical switches and miles of wire between the console and the wind chests. Finally it was finished, tuned, and I sat down and played a hymn at full organ. Fantastic! It was more wonderful than I had hoped.

In the meantime I had been scouting around for an organist. Our organist had been playing for a long time and wanted a rest. There was a very talented woman in Coos Bay whom I approached and promised her the job to play a pipe organ. She was an excellent one foot organist – meaning she played all the pedal notes with one foot which is typical when playing popular music. I promised I would teach her how to use both feet as well as the manipulation of the stops. She agreed. I felt she was a very brave person to have to learn a new technique and play in the presence of her teacher at the same time. She became a very good organist, and the time came when I could no longer help her. She went to the University of Oregon and continued to study. She has taught many young people in Coos Bay the art of the playing the pipe organ.

During the installation of the organ I discovered one of the workmen was gay. He suggested the next time I came to Portland I should look him up and he would introduce me to the gay bars and baths in the big city. Soon after his suggestion I went to Portland and took him up on his offer. We did the rounds. The bars became a refuge, a place to go when I was in Portland. In the bars I could be in the presence of others like myself. I could let down all the defenses which I had to use constantly in the straight world. If my wrist was a little limp, no one even noticed. Those moments became very important to me. Being in the presence of other gay men gave me an opportunity to begin to understand the meaning of being gay. They were moments of quietness within myself which helped me when I had to return to the straight world.

The baths were another refuge. They enabled me to take care of my sexual desires for men. Most gay men know it is next to impossible to turn off the sexual urge for another man. The advice of the psychiatrist in Oregon had been to be my gay self, and this was one way to do this. I could satisfy my sexual needs without too much guilt. Since we had agreed to handle our sexual needs in our own way, this was my choice. Having satisfied my sexual needs with a man also helped me perform sexually with my wife. I think she was aware that I had sexual contacts when I was out of town. I did not become totally impotent with my wife all at once. It slowly got worse as time went on.

There were times when nothing happened at the baths. Contrary to what many people think, gay men are not interested in having sex with every Tom, Dick, and Harry they meet. Most gay men are particular when choosing a sex partner and this was also true of me. One day at the baths I met a man and we were attracted to each other. We had a good time. When it was time for me to leave, he wanted to know my name and where I lived. No way! The blackmail incident was still too close and I would not let anyone know who I was or where I lived. At this time I was not thinking in terms of a divorce. I felt I was bisexual and all I needed was the opportunity now and then of fulfilling my sexual needs for a man. If there was no God-up-there keeping track of how often and how many men I had, the less guilty I felt. The issue was how well I handled my new found freedom in relation to my wife and to myself. I was not interested in finding a lover.

Outside of the theological journey, the remodeling, changing worship to Wednesday, the life of the congregation continued as usual. As far as I was concerned all things started anew in the life of the church. With a bit of apprehension I waited for the first Sunday after Labor Day. The program of the church would begin again and worship had returned to Sunday morning. Throughout the summer I wondered if there would be a drop in attendance come fall. The attendance would indicate whether or not I had gone too far since "That Sunday.". When I walked out of my office and into the chancel I was greatly relieved. The number of people sitting in the pews had not changed from Spring. This was reassuring. I hoped it was a sign the people were eager to see just where I would go with all of this. The usual programs of the church continued and outwardly we were like all other churches.

In the first six months I had learned it was easier to tear down, to destroy, than to replace and rebuild. I was quite sure that in time the No-God theologians would come up with some answers. They had not. The most difficult part of the journey was ahead. I remember how jealous I felt of the Israelites in the Old Testament. They had a cloud by day, pillar of fire by night, and footsteps in the sand. I felt we had nothing to guide us in our journey. But hindsight said to me, "Oh, Ye of little faith. Why did you think Yahweh would leave you without any guidance and direction?" I had not been able to see the help that was there. It had come in the ideas which would not leave my mind, and in taking the right continuing education classes. These were my footprints in the sand. They had been there but I was blind and had not noticed them. Like scripture, it was hindsight which enabled me to see I had had help.

Throughout the summer I wondered what I would do when fall arrived. I decided to introduce the congregation to Dietrich Bonhoeffer. He was a German pastor and theologian who lived during the Second World War. As a pastor he had discovered that the traditional approach of Christianity with its God-up-there did not meet the needs of his people. One phrase from Bonhoeffer's writings, *"The World has Come-of-Age,"* had caught the attention of the theological world. He felt that God was forcing us to live in a world in which God was not up-there or out-there. We (Christians) had become like young people who had outgrown the secure religious, moral and intellectual framework of our childhood. No longer could we meet the trials and temptations of life with the understanding the God-up-there was always available and ready to come to our aid. God was teaching us that we must live and get along very well without God. In Bonhoeffer's thinking we were faced with the difficulty of forgetting the God-up-there as the foundation of our faith, and learning to live without God because that was the only way in which God could be with us and help us. This was our introduction to the hiddenness of 'God.'

Another theologian who had an influence on me was Paul Tillich. He wrote a sermon entitled "The Depth of Existence." Here are a few ideas he had.

"The words 'deep' and 'depth' are used in our everyday lives in both a physical and spiritual manner. In poetry, philosophy and religious writing they indicate a spiritual attitude about ourselves. In the spiritual sense 'deep' is used as the opposite of 'shallow' or of 'high.' Truth is deep. Love is depth. Caring, concern, sharing all are deep aspects of our lives. But then, so are hate, anger, aggression.

"Most of us are enslaved by the routine of our daily lives. We are conquered by innumerable hazards, both good and evil. We are more driven than driving. We rush from one stop light only to have to wait at the next. Our hectic lives are like hit-and-run drives. We injure our souls by the rapidity with which we move on the surface itself; and then we rush away leaving our bleeding souls alone. We have no time for anything in life which goes below the surface until disaster strikes, shaking and disrupting our lives. Then we might be willing to look into the deeper aspect of our being.

"Most of us do not want to take the pains involved in getting beneath the surface of our lives. This is seen when sickness, pain, or trouble hits us and we blame the God-up-there. We seldom see these difficulties as an opportunity to look into the deeper aspect of our lives. A great naturalist was out in the countryside and came upon an emperor moth struggling to break its way through its cocoon. Taking his knife, the naturalist split the cocoon and released the moth from further struggle. The moth never developed, its wings never expanded, the color and tints that should have adorned never appeared. In the end it died, undeveloped, stunted, ruined.

"The depth of our lives is not something we fall into. It is something found by struggle, pain and effort. If we are to grown spiritually, we must look into the depth of our own lives sometime. When Tillich talks about a God 'down under' he is not reversing a God-up-there for one down-there. Tillich does not conceive of God as Being at all. He is talking about a depth of reality which is to be found at the very center of our lives, not on the surface where most of us play it."

While I wrestled with the idea of the ground and depth of our being, a phrase from my seminary days kept reminding me the meaning of good preaching and teaching. If I start in Jerusalem, I must end in Coos Bay, or if I start in Coos Bay, I must end up in Jerusalem. As far as I was concerned, the thinking of the theologians was important, but not as important as the Biblical message. I began with an exposition of the Exodus. It is primary in understanding the idea of God.

"The Exodus is the beginning of the history of Israel as a nation. This is not history in the ordinary sense. We are dealing with religious history. This means the events are subservient to the meaning behind the event. The hero of the Exodus was Moses. He was an Israelite who had been raised in the court of Pharaoh enjoying all of its rights and privileges. One day he got himself in deep trouble, he killed the Egyptian and had to flee for his own life. He became a refugee in the land of Midian. He was befriended by the Midianites and invited to live with them.

"One day while attending his father-in-law's sheep he saw a bush on fire, but the fire did not consume the bush. That burning bush certainly got the attention of Moses. He went over to the bush to see what was going on. As he came close a voice called to him, 'Moses, I have a job for you. I have seen the miserable condition of my people in Egypt, and I have decided to deliver them out of their misery You are the one to do this.'

"'Oh no, Lord, not me,' replied Moses. He did not feel he was important enough to be the recipient of God's message, to say nothing of being God's servant. Finally Moses was convinced he could not escape this call from 'The God of Abraham, Isaac, and Jacob,' and asked the Voice for his name. The answer, 'I am who I am.' (This is the translation of the Hebrew word, 'Yahweh'.) The Voice continued, 'If the sons of Israel want to know who sent you tell them "I Am" has sent me.' I can almost hear Moses say, 'thanks a whole bunch.'

"To the Hebrews, nothing was more important than a person's name. To know a person's name was to know all about him or her. Up until this time in the life of the tribes, their God had been known as the God of Abraham, Isaac and Jacob. This was not enough for Moses and wanting to know all about Yahweh Moses had asked the Voice his name. The answer given in the bush was terse and evasive. The request to know it all was denied. Instead the Voice demanded obedience, and by responding obediently, Moses would come to know Yahweh by what Yahweh would bring to pass. In other words, the question 'Who are you?' would be answered by the events that would transpire in the future. Yahweh was a hidden God, and Moses and his people, and people of all times would know 'I Am' through the events in history.

"Moses takes off for Egypt. Put yourself in Moses' place. You have been asked to do a job, but have not been given any credentials to present to the mighty Pharaoh. Moses was not in an enviable position. He had to return to the country from which he had fled. Surely he must have wondered what kind of reception would be waiting. Had the warrant for his arrest been lifted? He would find out. Apparently it had, because when he arrived in Egypt he was able to go into the court of Pharaoh without any harassment.

"Moses asked Pharaoh to let the Israelites go. Of course Pharaoh refused and a long confrontation between the two leaders began. This long contest was really a struggle between Yahweh, and the god of Egypt. Not until Egypt was visited by the Angel of Death did Pharaoh allow Moses and his people to leave. In the end Yahweh won, and Pharaoh allowed the people of Israel to leave. They had not been gone very long before Pharaoh came to his senses. Whatever possessed him to allow all that free, cheap labor to go? Pharaoh ordered his troops to give chase.

"Meantime those ex-slaves had reached the Sea-of-Weeds and were confronted with more water than they had ever seen and no way around. To make matters worse the Egyptian army was not far behind. The game was up. Those ex-slaves did not waste any time in letting Moses know of their great displeasure. They spent the night waiting for the worst to fall on them in the morning. In the morning they saw what appeared to be solid ground. They grabbed their possessions, started across the path, and discovered that the ground under their feet was not soft. In a short time they were on the other side. As the Egyptians gave chase, the wind stopped blowing, the tide came in and that took care of the Egyptians.

"Standing on the other side, pondering the events of their escape, Moses began to understand the meaning of 'I am.' Yahweh would be experienced in the historical events in Israel's life. Who would ever forget that crossing of the sea-of-weeds? Those ex-slaves would. Moses blew the whistle, the people lined up and before them were footprints in the sand. Where would they lead? Who knew? Who cared? They had assurances of the presence of Yahweh, a cloud by day and a pillar of fire by night. Their journey should have been a snap. They were free. What more could they want? In a few days they ran out of food and water. Did they remember their marvelous escape? No! They murmured. They complained. They said to Moses, 'We would be better off in the flesh pots of Egypt than to die out here in this forsaken wilderness.' The rest of their journey was filled with the difficulties they had in handling their freedom. In fact, as the rest of her history unfolds, Israel got the reputation of being a stiff-necked people. They discovered freedom to be a two-edged sword.

"What does all of this mean? Yahweh's activity lies outside the sacred institutions, and Yahweh's providence is revealed in all areas of life, the public as well as the private. There is a hiddenness to Yahweh, and this hiddenness stands at the very center of the doctrine of "God." It means Yahweh will disclose himself/herself at those places and in those ways he/she chooses, and not as we human beings want. In the process of disclosing himself/herself it is always different from how we humans would do it, but the disclosure is for human beings. What this means is Yahweh is not available for coercion and manipulation by human beings. No matter how religious we are, how persistent in our pleadings for help, we cannot force Yahweh to do our bidding."

It was easy to give the ideas in sermons, but to have a hidden God replace the Almighty God-up-there did not happen over night. It took many years for this idea to really become part of my life and the basis of my living. This book is the result of Yahweh who works behind the scenes not only in historical situations, but also in human relationships.

One day while visiting my daughter's children the conversation

53

made me realize that my grandchildren did not know their grandfather had been a minister most of his life. They had been born after I had left Coos Bay, and by the time they were aware of who their grandfather was, I was no longer pastor of a church. All they knew was I had a house cleaning business and on occasion helped their mother by cleaning her house. The very next day an inner urgency, something I cannot describe, made its message known. I knew I must write about my ministry in the Coos Bay Presbyterian church not only for my grandchildren, but for others as well. From that day until the book was finished I got up early in the morning, and there was no question as to what I would do. It was to work on the book. Fortunately I had written out most of the sermons given in Coos Bay which I still had and the Sunday bulletins which went with them. My memory also came to my rescue particularly in the personal aspects. This message comes to you through this human life with all of its strengths and weaknesses. Besides my grandchildren I want other people to have bread instead of the stones given out by the institutional churches.

The more I wrote, the more I knew I must write. As I was writing about the Exodus, the hiddenness of Yahweh, doubts began to assail me once again. No one else was talking about the hiddness of "I Am." Had I then, and was I now off on some tangent? One day shortly after I had started writing I remembered Elijah in the Old Testament. He had won the day for Yahweh against the priests of Baal, but then, for his safety, he had to flee and hide in a cave. He sat brooding and feeling sorry for himself, complaining to Yahweh that he was the only person in all of Israel who was still faithful. In the midst of his self-pity, "the still small voice of Yahweh" told Elijah there were more than three thousand faithful souls who had not bowed their knees to Baal, and he, Elijah, should stop feeling sorry for himself and get to work.(1) For fifteen years, I had been feeling sorry myself, when that Inner Presence told me, "Stop all that wallowing in self-pity. Get on with it. This you must do, so do it. There are people who want to hear what I have to say through you." The message of the Exodus, the hiddenness of "I Am' is not something way back there in the Old Testament. It is in the present.

A NEW CULTURE

Coos Bay was the ideal place to live if you liked to fish. There were small streams running through the valleys of the coastal range with Spring and Fall salmon runs and steelhead in the winter. Nearby lakes were filled with various kinds of pan fish. But I think for most people the most exciting fishing was on the ocean for salmon. Despite the fact my astrological sign is Pisces, I am not fond of water and fishing did not appeal to me. Someone once asked, "Don't you feel frustrated having all that great fishing available?" "No," I replied. "I would be frustrated if I liked to fish and did not have the time." My predecessor was in that position. He liked fishing. He was quite different from me. He was the kind of person who could walk into a room of complete strangers and in five minutes everyone felt as if they had been his friend all of their lives. I am a quiet person. I do not get pushy until I get to know you. Then, I might get a bit assertive. When it comes to theological matters I can be quite militant. In reality my predecessor was the pastor of the whole town, the whole county. I would be pastor of the First Presbyterian church in Coos Bay.

Although I did not care much for fishing, I was and still am an avid follower of professional football. Having been born and raised in Green Bay, Wisconsin, I have Packer blood running in my veins. When I arrived in Coos Bay, the Green Bay Packers were at the top of the football world under the leadership of Vince Lombardi. I used them as sermon illustrations on many an occasion, much to the chagrin of supporters of the Dallas Cowboys sitting in the pews. I did play tennis and I became a member of the Crooked

55

Brook Quash Club. It was a group of men who would get up and arrive at the tennis court at 6 a.m. for several sets of tennis. I was not the best player. At a Christmas party when various accolades were handed out, I was designated as the most graceful player. I was not the gung ho, masculine, macho type of man, and few straight men ever guessed I was gay. I liked music, and classical music in particular. I enjoyed pipe organ music, singing and directing choral music. I certainly was different from my predecessor. In time they would find out how different I really was.

In the fifties and sixties the experts told people it was important to take coffee breaks during the day. The people of Coos Bay took that to heart. When I arrived on the scene, I found there were small groups of people drinking coffee morning, noon and afternoon. The same people met at the same time and the same place. I became one of the regulars at several of those gatherings. I felt being present at the coffee breaks was important. It enabled me to get a pulse on what was happening in the community. It gave me the opportunity to show them I was not the typical man of the cloth. I was not tied to the sanctuary of the church building. I was not up in some ivory tower. I was part of the world. If I walked in and someone was in the middle of telling an off-color joke, I did not want them to quickly change the subject as they did when other ministers came in. I enjoyed those jokes as well as they did. I was willing to let them know that men of the cloth also entertained such ideas, and were not that easily offended.

One group consisted primarily of business men, members of the fire department, city officials and a few others. Most of the conversation centered on sports, local news and mostly chitchat. One day the assistant chief of the fire department made some snide remark about a player on the Blazer basketball team. He implied the player might have played a better game if he did not have an interest in men off the court as well as on the court. After listening to this for a while and taking the chance of guilt by association, I suggested that I did not see how his interest in men would affect his ability to play basketball. The assistant fire chief did not agree and continued his accusations. I stood my ground. It was the theological ideas I was preaching, besides the social aspect of drinking coffee, which made me be in the community. If God is growth, change, history, politics and is at work in this world and not bound to the sanctuary, it was important that I be present at the coffee groups.

"Well, what was happening on the home front?" In one of my sessions with the psychiatrist I mentioned that before the blackmail incident, when our daughter had become sick, I had told my wife about my interest in men. He pointed out that when I had done that I had decided within myself I wanted to get out of the marriage sometime or other. Since he had suggested from the very beginning of our sessions that I should accept my being gay, the direction of my life changed. Trying to accept being a gay man and living that life was not easy. Trying to fulfill some of the needs of being gay and appearing to be straight was not easy. It certainly did not solve being impotent with my wife. It did create an interesting situation in my life.

I felt free to fulfill my need to have sexual encounters with men. When I had had sex with a man, I felt the need to have sex with my wife. I would have sex with her, and then, I wanted to have a man. Back and forth it went. When with one, I wanted the other. At first I found this to be interesting, but then it turned into a merry-go-round. As this continued I began to realize that being with a man was more fulfilling, more satisfying, more complete. The fact of being gay was beginning to assert itself. One day I said to myself, "Hannon, let's face it. When you go looking for a sexual partner you are only interested in finding a man not a woman. It is time you accept the fact that you are not bisexual, you are gay and that is that."

That decision had an affect on my married life. Exploring sexuality with men was coming to terms with myself, but it did not help my being impotent with my wife. The impotence slowly began to get worse. I tried to compensate, but compensation will only go so far. The sexuality between us became less and less. There really was nothing either of us could do about it. Our life together was not a total bore. There were many good times. We had a circle of friends and spent many happy hours with them. In their presence we could forget our problems and look like any other happily married couple. We tried to do the best we could in the impossible situation of my having to live a lie.

Living a double life is a pain in the neck. My acceptance of my gayness really did not solve much of anything. The world in which I lived did not accept it. Certainly the Presbyterian Church, as a denomination, did not accept it. Going back and forth between a man and my wife was getting me nowhere. Talk about being depressed. I was. In fact the psychiatrist had me on medication to help handle my depression. One answer I considered was suicide. I thought about it mostly when I was depressed and driving home from a meeting. If I committed suicide my wife would be free of me, and no one would know what kind of man she had married.

It would have been so easy. Returning home late at night from a church meeting I could run into a bridge abutment. There, that would do it. Both of us would get off free. Only trouble with that idea, I would not be around. I did not harbor such thoughts for any length of time but they did come on more than one occasion. When suicide did come into my mind I entertained the thought for a while and then decided there had to be another way. Sometimes the advice of my psychiatrist came to mind. Depression is aggression turned inward. I resolved to learn how to handle it.

For me celibacy was not an answer. If I had tried that I am sure I would have become mentally ill. The idea of finding a man for a long-time relationship began to take shape. Even cruising took on a different purpose. From just looking for sex, to looking for Mr. Wonderful. About this time I discovered other gay men in Coos Bay, but not Mr. Wonderful and that was okay. If I had met Mr. Wonderful, he would have presented a situation I was not ready to face. Most of the men I met were married. We were all in the same boat. There was an unwritten law in Coos Bay that if you met another man on the street you knew was gay, you protected that knowledge. If you were both alone you would nod, say "Hi," maybe chitchat for a few moments, or even have a cup of coffee. If he was in the company of others who might be family, you did not recognize him.

As there had been a change in my life, it was time to change the metaphor in the life of the congregation. Israel's journey had been in the wilderness of Sinai. I did not ask the members of the congregation to take off with me and spend some time in the semi-desert country of Eastern Oregon. They would not have followed even if I had suggested it. The journey of the congregation of the Coos Bay Presbyterian church would take place in a entirely different setting. The Secular Society, as a world view, was coming into its own following the Second World War. The influence of the secularization process was being felt and experienced even in the small towns and hamlets of our nation, and Coos Bay was no exception. This happened through that instrument, the television set. It brought the rest of the world into our living rooms and we could see, hear and experience events throughout the world.

Robert R and I were returning from some meeting and were talking about the impact of television on our lives. Television was the symbol of a whole new technological world that was fast engulfing us. I suggested that the basis of this technology was very Biblical.
  "You have to be kidding," said Robert.
  "No," I replied.

"I suppose we are going to hear about this in some sermons?"
"You got it," I replied and started the following Sunday.

"For ages the only real enemy the institutional church ever sighted in the woods was the worldly world. Many a preacher clobbered the world for being itself, worldly. Now we must stop. This secular world in which we live is our baby, and it is high time we stop trashing it. Arab traders have been engaged in commerce for centuries, but they did not create the modern international money market. Indian philosophy and religious thinking have had a longer, more distinguished continuous history than anything in Europe, but Indian philosophy did not create the modern cosmopolitan university. The Chinese were centuries ahead of Europe in several important mechanical developments, but they did not produce the modern international standards of technology. Even though the development of the modern world civilization was the product of Western Europe it was not due to any special endowment of skill or intelligence. There is good reason to believe that the rise of modern science and technology was related to some basic beliefs about the natural world and the place of human beings in it that are distinctive in the Bible.

"Harvey Cox developed similar ideas in his book, *The Secular City*. He explored the relationship between the emerging secular society and certain basic concepts in the Bible. Secularization withdrew areas of life, thought patterns and activity from the control of religious bodies, that were believed to be revealed religious truths. On the plus side it was seen as the increasing assertion of the competence of human science and techniques to handle human problems of every kind. From the Biblical point of view human beings were now able to enter into the freedom given to us in the Christ. This freedom delivered human beings from the control of all other powers and gave them mastery of the created world that was promised to humankind in the Exodus.

"The great characteristic of secularization is pluralism, which is becoming an important part in American culture. The problem is the role of being religious has fallen to the Christians. The church is expected to play the medicine-man role and a prophetic role at the same time. Not possible. If the institutional churches will look at Japan, one of the most secular and pluralistic societies, they will discover a person will drive past three or four temples and at least one Shinto shrine on their way to a Christian church. The Christian in Japan has always known and lived in pluralism. The Japanese Christians are in a better position than we, because they can turn the jazz and garbage of being religious to the other religions. The other religions can bless home plate and leave the church functioning as the Christ in society. Pluralism is the kissing cousin of secularization.

"The Exodus is the basis of our secular society because it emphasizes that no person rules by divine right in a secular city. Pharaoh was the ruler of Egypt because he was a descendent of Ra, the sun-god. Therefore, not only was Pharaoh king, he was king because divine blood ran through his veins. Who could challenge such a sacred right to rule? Well, along came Moses. He did. When Moses could not persuade Pharaoh to let his people go, the only action left was to lead the Israelites out of Egypt. The Exodus could be interpreted as an act of insurrection against a duly constituted monarch.

"The Exodus made it impossible for any monarch to claim the right to rule because of divine blood in his veins. Yahweh could always stage a new Exodus, or work through history to bring down any monarch or system with delusions of grandeur. Yet Israel in her own time and place tried the same thing. The oldest and broadest swath of Old Testament writing is about the monarch and King David.

61

The climax came when Nathan, the prophet, entered the palace, pointed his finger at David and denounced his affair with Bathsheba. The anointing of David to be Yahweh's king had not given him freedom to do as he pleased with the lives of his subjects. David did not protest either the accusation of Nathan or the judgment pronounced on him. The state has only a provisional worth, and that is one condition no tyrant can stand.

"In the New Testament the early Christians would pray for the emperor but would not burn incense on his altar. To pray for the emperor was to grant him the right to exercise authority over them in a particular restricted way. To refuse to put incense on his altar was to deny him any sacred claims to the office. Yet, as the church grew in power in the Middle Ages, the Pope tried to establish his right to rule over all of Christendom. It did not work. Any attempt to return to simple sacred politics is futile. This opens a world filled with new possibilities for political and social change.

"Another basis for the process of secularization is found in the Ten Words. (The Ten Commandments) It is based on the prohibition against the making of any graven images of Yahweh. To the people of that time, gods and value systems were one and the same. The prohibition against making graven images, from the point of view of the Israelites, was that nothing which they or any human being could fashion out of physical material could have any real moral significance. The Israelites did not feel making an idol might cheapen or mislead religious worship. They believed that it was impossible to make any replication of Yahweh by human effort, and any deity which could be expressed in the form of an idol was in fact not Yahweh. The Bible does not deny the reality of the gods and their value systems represented by an idol. It merely relativizes them and accepts them as the result of human hands.

"There is danger in this concept. It may lead to ethical

anarchism. We may use our new found freedom not to become true human beings, but to revel in all of the things the dead leader once forbade. If Christ has set us free from the dominion of any and all powers, then as Christians we are willing to relativize values so can they be themselves. For example in the receiving of the covenant, Israel's set of values would be more humane. Israel would have a different, more humane set of values than her neighbors. Israel would have an eye for and eye and a tooth for a tooth. This would make life more humane because the moral systems of her neighbors allow them to take a whole life if a person had lost only an eye. In time Jesus came along relativized everything and threw the moral standards of the Pharisees into total confusion. From the Christian point of view our morality can only be in the context of 'agape' (love) enabling us to form a basis for living in this world.

"The third Biblical basis for secularization is found in the idea of creation. There is a great difference between the Hebrew writer's use of the creation stories and their use by the Sumerian, Egyptian, and Babylonian cultures. To those people magic was a world view and not simply someone doing tricks before their eyes. Primitive people saw their world as a system in which they were related to everything within their world and these cultures saw the sun, moon, and stars as semi-gods. Both god and humanity were part of nature, and the society in which humanity lived was bound under nature, time and space.

"This is why the Hebrew view of Creation signaled such a marked departure from the surrounding cultures. It is designed to teach the Hebrews that the magical idea – the sun, moon, and the stars as semi-divines partaking of the divinity of the gods themselves – is not so. In Genesis, Yahweh hung the sun and moon in the sky to light the world for humans; they are neither gods or semi-divine beings. The stars have no control over a person's life because they are made by Yahweh. None of the heavenly bodies can make any claim to religious awe or worship so do not waste your time on your horoscope. Our ties as human beings are not with nature. They reach back to the histories of our forefathers, and forward into the future of our children's children. We are free to be human beings, and nature is free to be nature.

"This means we should not confuse 'God' with the trees. They are 'God's' trees, but they are not God. Cut them down. Make houses out of them, not idols. The thrust of the Creation story in the Bible is to free us from the taboos and semi-religious nature of the other religions and cultures of that time. In Genesis human beings are freed to be human. Nature is nature, and only out of this kind of situation can natural science arise. This took place within Western Christian culture, not in any other culture.

"Secularization opens up the possibilities of new freedom and of new enslavement for us. As secularization gains in acceptance it is creating a world in which it is easy to forget God, to give up all traditional religious practices, and consequently lose all sense of meaning and purpose in life. It is not the mission of the church to look at the dark side and to offer the Gospel as an antidote to disillusionment, but rather to see secularization is our baby. Do not clobber it, understand it, and in the light of the scriptures, live for it through Yahweh. That is our task as Christians."

Despite the theological content of the sermons, I did not make many changes in the program of the congregation or in worship. I made one suggestion and it was in the realm of worship. In the Presbyterian Church, Maundy Thursday (the Thursday before Easter) is traditionally a time to celebrate communion. Usually this service centers on the events of the last days of Jesus, and ends with the serving of communion.

The Gospels say that Jesus wanted to celebrate the Passover with his disciples, but the incidents described indicate it was not the Passover they celebrated but rather another meal. It was common in Jesus' day for a teacher to have a group of followers who were known as an Haburah. The events that are described in the Gospels are not the observance of the Passover, but rather a meal in which the ties of fellowship and the bonds of love that tied the Haburah together were celebrated. The details given in the Gospels describe a fellowship meal with Jesus functioning as the host, and performing all of the duties of the host. He did not pass these duties off to a servant. When the disciples arrived Jesus washed their feet. In Jesus's day the washing of feet was what any good host would do to make his guests feel comfortable and at home. (1)

With this in mind I suggested that on Maundy Thursday our communion service be more in keeping with these ideas. We would begin with dinner. The members of the Session would serve as the host and bring the main dish. The members of the congregation would bring either a green salad or apple pie. Only members of the congregation were invited to this service.

As the members arrived they were greeted by a member of the Session and served a nonalcoholic drink. I had wanted to serve wine but did not have the courage to do so. (This was our version of the washing of feet.) Our members all wore good shoes. Therefore, as good hosts we did not need to wash feet. Instead we greeted one another in the manner of our time and served a drink. After the members had arrived, we went into the Fellowship hall and sat around tables. Each table had a Session member who, as the host, served the meal. It was suggested the conversation around each table concern itself with the meaning of the Christian faith or any question anyone had concerning the spiritual journey we had undertaken.

Following the common meal, I stood up and read the communion service. Then I took a piece of bread, broke it and handed it to the person next to me, who broke it, and handed it to the next person. The elder at each table did the same thing. This was followed by the drinking of coffee, the common drink of our time. This was better than grape juice. We then moved into the sanctuary for the singing of appropriate hymns and the reading of scripture passages taking us through Gethsemane and Good Friday. We left the sanctuary in silence, until we would return on Easter Sunday. This became our observance of Maunday Thursday as long as I was pastor.

No further changes in the form of worship took place for some time. I guess I felt the challenge of the sermons was disturbing enough. I was distressed because the No-God theologians had not come up with a new name for "God." I felt stranded. So intent had I been on finding a new name for "God" I had not listened to my own sermons. If "I Am" was not going to give Moses a name, who was I to expect a new name. I had come to a dead end on the doctrine of "God." That was good. I was forced to look in another direction.

There were some changes in the life of the congregation. The church school, the women's association and the youth program were still functioning. But there were some indications all was not well. Our financial situation was not good. That is one of the first signs that the minister is in trouble. The Session addressed the problem, the money we needed was given and we ended the year with money to pay our debts.

A second indication of trouble was attendance on Sunday morning. On "That Sunday." we had had two services with 87 people attending the first service and 102 the second. As we continued on our journey attendance at the second service had continued to decline and the Session decided to drop it after a year and a half.

We had a single service with about 130 people . This drop in attendance was difficult for me to accept. I was very aware that some of the members, who had clapped the hardest when the journey began, had dropped out along the way. Apparently the new theological ideas had been too much. From my perspective this was very frustrating. I had finally found some meaningful answers to the Christian faith. If I liked what I had found, why did they not like it as well? I had forgotten that the motive for the life of Jesus was the Suffering Servant of the Lord. I did not think that applied to me. It did. I did not like it.

"That Sunday" was now in the past. From hindsight I can see there had been footprints in the sand only I had not recognized them. I was being lead in a different direction. The focus was not to be on the doctrine of God. It was to be on the life of Jesus. I would soon be exposed to some very exciting and wonderful ideas about the essence of the Christian faith.

WALKING ON WATER

I attended a traveling seminar at the First Presbyterian Church in Medford given by professors from the San Francisco Theological Seminary. When Professor Herman C. Waetjen entered the room and began his lectures I was in for the shock of my life. He was younger than I was. "No way," I thought, "professors are always much older than their students. Look again, Hannon. That man is younger than you. Take that." The real shock was that I was face to face with the fact that I had passed the BIG FORTY in my life. I just did not want to admit I was no longer young. I took hold of myself and listened carefully and took copious notes of what he said and I still have them. The lectures were on the resurrection, and what I received from them became a powerful influence in my life, and for many of the people in the congregation. Here is what I received from Professor Waetjen, what I gave and what I believe.

67

"Central to the Christian faith is Easter. For many people it is the annual renewal of their religious insurance policy. They like being reassured that Jesus rose from the dead, and they can count on a resurrection for themselves, somehow, somewhere, someplace. Not so! In the New Testament the Easter event has more to do with the meaning of our lives in the here and now than what happens after we die. When the resurrection did happen, the disciples were not psychologically prepared for what took place. A crucified and dead Messiah did not make any sense. Confronted by the risen Lord, they were dumbfounded. For the moment, the resurrection blotted out everything else in the mind of the early church. The fact that the resurrection put the rest of Jesus' life out of focus is probably the best proof we have that it did occur. The Christian faith is based on the fact of the resurrection, not on how it took place. The sources do not tell us how the resurrection happened. The 'how' is not as important as the 'meaning.' Most important are the conclusions the disciples drew from that event.

"Our clue to understanding the Easter Event comes from the preaching of the early church. In the book of Acts the message does not emphasize life after death. The people of that time already believed that. The disciples are proclaiming this Jesus is no longer just their teacher, now he is the Christ. This man Jesus was truly the Son of God. They would never again be able to remember the life of Jesus, as Jesus the man. Now they see him and think of him as the Christ. Despite this, they were so unprepared for the resurrection, they did not know what to make of it.

"In the twenty-first chapter of the Gospel of John we find the disciples have returned to their fishing business. They had been confronted by the risen Lord prior to this meeting but did not think their lives would be any different. They had taken off and gone back to their former way of living.

Jesus appeared once again and says, 'Sorry about that boys, but it just cannot be. The fishing business is not for you. Faith is not sitting around and waiting, it is activity and work. Just as the disciples were about to sink back into their old ways, Jesus, who is now the Christ, comes and says, 'You are mine; you are part of my body, the church, and as Yahweh is working, and I am working, so also do I call you to live for me in this world.'

"The preaching of the early church proclaimed that Jesus had been crucified by lawless people, but Yahweh had raised him from the dead and made him both Christ and Lord. The resurrection was Yahweh's stamp of approval on the life and work of Jesus. The disciples no longer call him teacher, or prophet. He is 'the Christ and Lord.' In the life, death and resurrection of this man, Jesus, they had seen Yahweh defined in human terms. Jesus was more than any other person had ever been and the disciples conferred on him the title 'The Christ.' Easter's message involves our existence as men and women living within history. It is something offered to us who are willing to die to this world, so that we can be raised up into the life of Yahweh in the midst of this world.

"In the resurrection something happened in the world which caused a fundamental change. We are just beginning to understand this. Resurrection is historical existence. In the drama 'Prometheus Bound' we find the basic ideas of the Greeks. Prometheus was a primeval deity who raided heaven and stole fire from the gods. He brought it back to earth and gave it to humanity. As a gift fire was a blessing. It enabled humanity to begin the arts and crafts of civilization. But the gods were angry. Prometheus must be punished. The punishment handed out by Zeus was to chain Prometheus to a rock. Every day an eagle would come, eat out his liver, and during the night the liver would grow back. The next day the same event would take place, and this went on forever.

"The gods are angry because Prometheus has transgressed the fundamental law of the universe. The Greeks believed that all of the world was divided into spaces, and those spaces were separated by boundary lines. A person had to live their life within the set boundary lines. They could not step over them. As soon as a person did, they would be faced with their destiny. Destiny was that force which handed out punishment for any injustice or transgression. The Greeks were taught by their religious attitude toward life that they must confine their existence within the fundamental structures of the law. The law, therefore, was basic. The law was absolute. Life was a balance and a person made sure that they did not overstep the boundary lines. If you did, you either met one of the gods who would punish you, or you met your destiny which would do the same.

"The resurrection shatters this kind of thinking. It presents a fantastic breakthrough in the lives of human beings and their relationship to the Divine. There are two incidents in the Gospel of Matthew which help us understand this difference between Greek thinking and that of the early Christian Church. In the eighth chapter Jesus and his disciples are in a boat. Jesus has fallen asleep. In the midst of this enjoyable ride, a great storm suddenly came swooping down on them. Matthew says it was caused by an earthquake. He wants the reader to be aware that this is not just any ordinary storm. The disciples are terrified and not really interested in drowning. They shake Jesus and wake him up. Jesus stands up and calms the storm.

"This is more than a so-called miracle story. It is more than just narrative. This is the theology of the writer of the Gospel of Matthew. The sea is a symbol of the forces of chaos which threaten the little group of disciples in their boat. This is a picture of the early church caught up in the violence of the world in which they live. In this incident Jesus is with the church. At the pleading of the disciples, he stands up and calms the elements. Therefore, Jesus is Lord of the universe. He is Lord over chaos. Jesus functions as Yahweh did in the Old Testament taking care of the needs of Israel and protecting them. In return they were to live in a relationship to Yahweh and to each other through the observance of the law that had been given.

"Turning to the fourteenth chapter of Matthew we find another story of Jesus, the disciples and a storm. (Most New Testament scholars agree that this is a resurrection appearance of Jesus which the writer put in the gospel, before the resurrection happened.) Jesus has sent his disciples ahead while he remained on the mountain to pray. The disciples are in a boat trying to reach the other side. Things are not going well. They are battling another storm. In the midst of their struggle, they look up and are confronted by a man walking on the water. They are so shaken by what appears to be a ghost, they cry out in terror. Jesus calms them. Then Peter says, 'Lord, if it is you, command me to come to you on the waters.' Jesus says, 'Come.' Peter gets out of the boat and walks on water. That Peter succeeded before he failed is something we often forget. (1)

"Traditional preaching has emphasized the fact that he began to sink and needed to be saved. We should not forget that Peter did get out of the boat. He did walk on water. He succeeded before he failed, and that is what is important. Peter leaves the security of the boat and engages in the impossible. He rises above the laws of nature. In this account in Matthew we find Peter doing the very thing that humans were not supposed to do according to the Greeks. Peter is rising above the laws of nature and does not meet his destiny! He is not punished as Prometheus was.

"There is a difference between this story and the previous

71

one in Matthew. In the first one, Jesus does everything for his disciples as Yahweh had done for Israel. But in the second, Jesus comes to his disciples. In response to the command, 'Come,' Peter gets out of the boat and walks on water. This is where the New Testament is different from the Old Testament. In the resurrection of Jesus, the Christ, we have a fundamental change in the structure of the universe. Because of the resurrection it is now possible for human beings to rise above and transcend the limitations the Greeks thought were there. Peter risks insecurity, even death by getting out of the boat. He confronts the elements, dares to take the challenge and in so doing participates in the Lordship of Jesus, the Christ.

"This is the message of the New Testament. This is the message of the resurrection. Peter represents every Christian, and the Christ calls to every Christian, 'Come.' He calls us to leave the security of the boat, step out and start walking on water. He calls us to battle against the seemingly over-powering forces of society. Jesus is Lord even of that, and we participate with him in this Lordship. This is the only way human beings can truly become human.

"The resurrection is not running away from living in the midst of history. It is creating order out of disorder, tearing down and building up structures. Yahweh recognizes and accepts the things which we do. The resurrection says we can rise above the powers of the world in which we live because we participate with the risen Lord in the Lordship over this world.

"If the resurrection means getting out of the boat, then every time we do this we are taking a gamble. We are always facing risks. Our response may be right or wrong. As far as Yahweh is concerned what really matters is not whether we are right or wrong, but whether we have taken the risks.

"The characteristic verb in both the Old and New

Testaments is the 'comingness' of Yahweh. Or to put it another way, Yahweh is always one step ahead of us, beckoning us to come from where we are to where Yahweh is. The same idea is found in the resurrection account in the gospel of Mark. When the disciples came to the empty tomb, the young man who was sitting there told them that Jesus was on his way to Galilee. If they wanted to encounter the risen Lord; they would not find him in the sacred ghetto of Jerusalem, but out in the world. This is true for us. We will not meet the risen Christ in any sanctuary on Easter Sunday, but when we bump shoulders with another, an acquaintance, with a stranger that encounter might be the risen Christ coming to us. The Christ is just that intangible.

"This does not mean every encounter with another person is a meeting with the risen Christ. It means that we never know at what time or under what conditions the Christ comes. It is also possible that we may be the Christ to another person. This idea of the Christ and Yahweh being known in interpersonal encounters is difficult to grasp. We have not been taught to think in this manner. We have been taught that if we can get into the right religious posture, atmosphere, or perhaps to some holy shrine, we might luck out and experience the Risen Christ.

"Somewhere I read that Dostoevsky, the great Russian novelist, desperately wanted a vision of the Christ. He felt it would be important to him in his writing. One day he came upon a small country church. He went in and assumed the position of prayer. A man came and knelt beside him. Dostoevsky did not turn, but he was sure the man kneeling beside him was the Christ. Finally he made an effort and looked at the man. He saw a face, like every peasant's face. 'What sort of Christ is this?' thought Dostoevsky. 'Such an ordinary man; it cannot be.' He started to turn away, but before he had finished, he was convinced the Christ was kneeling next to him. Only then did he realize that such a face was the face of the Christ, the face of any person. The Christ is just that intangible. We never know when or where we will meet the Christ."

The idea of getting out of the boat and facing the terrors of life became the basis and strength of my eventually coming out in Coos Bay, in Presbytery, and finally to a committee of the General Assembly. When I first comtemplated writing I thought of writing a commentary on the important passages in the Bible for gays and lesbians. But on second thought to interpret Biblical passages just for gays and lesbians would support the idea that we are very different from other people which is not true. We are human beings first and foremost, and our lives are filled with the same joys, fulfillment's, ambitions as anyone else. They are also filled with pain, anguish, unfulfilled hopes and dreams. We differ from the straight world only in our sexual orientation, which produces subtle influences on us, but does not require interpreting the Bible just for us.

The message of the Christian faith is for people regardless of their sexual orientation. This idea of the resurrection – getting out of the boat, walking on water – is one that speaks to the gay and lesbian community about getting out of the closet. The call of Jesus, the Christ, is, "Come, leave the security of your closet. Be yourself, the gay man or lesbian woman you are. As long as you remain in the closet, life will continue as usual. You hope no one will find out about your sexual orientation and you will be safe. As Matthew had to leave his tax-gathering place, and Peter had to get out of the boat, so you must leave the apparent security of the closet. As long as you remain in the closet, the relative security can always be exposed. Someone somewhere can let out the word. "He is gay! She is lesbian! See, I told you so." Your life is shattered. The safety of the closet has crumbled. It was not safe after all.

As long as you remain in the closet, you close the door on your own growth as a person, and certainly in your spirit. The call of the Christ is to get out of the boat and battle with the forces of this world, which can be deadly, but it is a call to the wholeness and fullness of your life. When you get out of the boat you are not on your own, the risen Christ is also there. If you have chosen the right congregation, you will be accepted and supported. If not, then find the right one. Faith is not sitting around and waiting for something to happen. As gay men, and lesbian women you must rise and follow him.

The messages of "Getting out of the boat" and "walking on water" had caught the imaginations of those who had heard those sermons, and soon they injected them in their conversations. This meaning of the resurrection had made its impression and became important in the lives of many of the members.

The renewed willingness to discuss spiritual matters grew beyond the church as well. Robert R. and a few other members of the church suggested I become a member of the Lions Club. I attended the weekly meetings content just to sit and listen, but at one meeting the man sitting opposite me started a conversation about a person's idea of God. Of course I was always ready for such an encounter and launched into it with great fervor. The person setting next to the man to whom I was talking listened for a while and then stood up. He called to get the president's attention and accused me of advertising. This was not allowed at a Lion's meeting. He demanded I be fined. I immediately rose and said, "Anytime I have a chance to save a soul, I would gladly pay a fine." I paid my fine. A dime.

The discussion with the man had centered on the difficulty we all have when speaking about God. The man was a faithful member of another church, but he was not getting any answers to his questions concerning God. His clergy kept bypassing his

75

questions. I did not. He was puzzled and asked, "Why do people still go to church when their questions are not being answered?"

I replicd, "For many people the church is the last great fortress against all the encroaching pressures in our world. Many people seek safety behind the walls of the sanctuary so they do not have to face life. They have been taught they will find God in a little red light hanging in the chancel. They have forgotten the teaching of Jesus, 'He/she who would seek to save his/her life from involvement in this world will surely lose it, and only he/she who is willing to lose his/her life involved in the world will find it.'" (2)

As a result of this discussion, this man plus a few other men in the community, members of other churches, began meeting with me to discuss John Robinson's book, *Honest to God*. This book had been important to me because Robinson not only raised the issue of God, but he asked other questions about some of the traditional ideas of the Christian faith, questions which these men were asking themselves. The sessions were held in the Elk's Lodge once a week. Once again the importance of my being present in the life of Coos Bay was reaffirmed. Many of these men were also in some of the coffee groups which met every day. My presence meant more than being just another coffee drinker; it often gave me an opportunity to meet the needs of others.

After meeting with this group for a while I talked about the cost of being a disciple. Not every person who hears the call responds in the positive.

"The call of Jesus, the Christ, comes to all people, but not everyone responds, 'Okay, Lord, here I am.' In the gospel of Mark we have the story of the rich young ruler. Translated into our time he would be a young man just a few years out of college. At this early age he is already successful. He is the Junior Chamber of Commerce Man of the Year. He is

the most eligible bachelor in town. He has everything going for him. He is the clean-cut all-American-boy who has made a success of his life while still young. What more could anyone ask? The young ruler comes to Jesus with the question, 'What must I do to inherit eternal life?' Jesus looks straight at him; his heart warmed to him and he says, 'One thing you lack: go, sell everything you have and give to the poor and you will have riches in heaven. Come follow me.'
(3)At these words the young man's face fell and he went away with a heavy heart. He was a man of great wealth
"The young man could not believe what he had heard. In Jesus' day riches demonstrated divine favor. Poverty meant divine disfavor. Money is not the issue. The issue is spiritual. As far as Jesus was concerned the man's life would not be complete until he was willing to leave the security of all his possessions, and risk the insecurity of living in the presence of Jesus. Compared to Peter in the boat, the storm, getting out and walking on water, this young man did not have the courage to pay the price. He preferred security. He preferred to play it safe. He turned and walked away, and we hear of him no more. All of us are presented with the same choice. 'What is there in my life which I must give up, which prevents me from getting out of the boat and following the Christ? There is a demand to following the Christ. The question each one of us must ask ourselves is, Are we willing to pay the price?"

In the meantime summer had arrived, and I decided to attend "The Seminary-in-the-Mountains." It had been advertised as a time for the minister to study with his wife and family. I decided to take my children with me. It would give us some time together, and my wife would have some time for herself without the responsibility of the family. When my children and I arrived at the conference, we cause a bit of a stir. The other ministers had arrived with their families. I had my children but not my wife. Someone asked

"Why?" I replied, "To give my wife some time free from the responsibilities of the family." Several of the other wives gave their husbands a look indicating they liked the idea; why hadn't their husbands thought of it?

It was a good time for my children and myself. They were junior high age and we got to do things we did not have time to do during the school year. Even though we lived in the midst of the lumber industry, we had not been to a lumber mill. We had the chance and took it. It was interesting but not the most exciting event during the conference. Near by was a ski resort, and one afternoon we took the ski lift up to the top. That ride was quite different in summer. There was a long, long distance between our dangling feet and the ground. When we got to the top I discovered my son did not like heights. We returned to the bottom as soon as possible. While the adults were having classes, the children were engaged in activities. At meal time I sat with my children because we were a family, and meal times were a time for us to be together. Other children would join us, and I took great delight in teasing all of them. Often there was much laughter at our table while the rest of the adults ate their meals. We had a good time at that conference and returned to Coos Bay energized. Fall would soon be upon us and life would return to normal, or would it?

ADRIFT

Challenging many of the sacred doctrines of traditional Christianity had been very exciting in the beginning. Although we had found some new answers, there were unanswered questions. I was not sure where I would find the answers, and that left me with the feeling of being more or less adrift. I was not sure where this journey would lead us.

When the congregation's life returned to normal in September we instituted the "Talk-back." As the coffee hour was coming to an end I would announce that the "Talk-back" would begin. It was a forum that provided an opportunity for the people to ask questions raised by the morning's sermon, or past sermons or any issue on anyone's mind. It also provided an opportunity for the members to be in dialogue with me and each other. Following a sermon on prayer, someone suggested I had not been very clear, so I tried again a few weeks later.

I said that prayer was not closing our eyes, folding our hands and having a monologue with the God-up-there. Prayer was the coming together of two persons in unconditional love toward each other. This means if we are having a cup of coffee with someone and we get beyond the usual chit chat and into an honest struggle of importance to one or both, that is prayer. When we seek to be with another at the depth of our being, whether in silence, or action, that is prayer. Prayer is the responsibility to meet others with all I am. If that happened both persons would be in the presence of God, the heart of intercessory prayer.

This led to a change in our worship. The morning prayer, sometimes called the pastoral prayer, was changed from a monologue by the minister telling the God-up-there, all that was wrong in the world to a participatory "concerns of the church," a time when the members of the congregation could voice matters important to them. Sometimes the concerns were personal, but most of the time they were of a social nature. This was followed by a time of silence while the people reflected on the concerns which had been expressed, or matters important to them. In a striking example of this new open communication, some people had objected to the language of the Lord's prayer. They felt many of the words were not consistent with the theological ideas we had encountered in our journey. I decided I would not use the Lord's prayer.

Another development in the life of the congregation that autumn was the formation of new adult study groups. They were important because the context of many sermons had first been explored in the adult discussion groups. I felt if the people in the pews on Sunday were to make any sense of what they heard on Sunday morning it would benefit them to be part of a group. The groups had a specific format. They were composed of eight to twelve people. In that size group even the most shy people usually felt free to express themselves or to ask questions.

As the people arrived for the study groups they shared a glass of wine and caught up on the latest gossip. This was followed by a planned pot-luck dinner. I felt that in this sharing of a meal an unknown presence was there. Following the meal I usually interpreted a passage of scripture, followed by questions and discussion. The scripture passages were familiar, but I had a new understanding which had come from my continuing education. Often their response was, "Here we go again." Sometimes the members asked questions which had been running around in their heads. In that case whatever I had prepared for the evening was set aside and their concern was discussed. In a real sense these people were involved in our theological journey.

While we were losing some members, we were gaining others. Our approach was getting the attention of young couples with backgrounds in college, where many of them had been taught to question all traditional organizations and authority. Since I was questioning the traditional stance of the institutional church, they were attracted to what I was saying. Many of the new members came to the church through their participation in an adult discussion group.

One October I attended a Pastor-In-Residence Fall Seminar at San Francisco Theological Seminary. During the day the participating clergy were free to attend classes, read or do whatever we wanted.

In the evening we spent time with one of the professors. I took a class on the problems of Christology. That rather foreboding sounding title simply meant a study of the identity of Jesus and his relationship to God. There were four of us in the class, just the right number of people. After the third day we realized our traditional concepts of Jesus were being challenged.

One evening we began to talk about how our congregations would accept the shift we were making and the changes they would have to make. The other ministers were anxious about the response of their members, but I said, "I'll simply get up Sunday morning and say, 'Get ready, we've got to shift again.'" It became clear during the week that no matter what I thought I knew about the Christian faith, I was in for new ideas and thoughts which would burst any treasured theology I still held dear to my heart.

This seminar was led by Professor Herman C. Waetjen whose earlier lectures had exposed me to the idea of resurrection as getting out of the boat and walking on water, an idea which had become a foundation of my Christian faith. In this seminar we explored the Christian message in current novels. We were asked to read *One Flew Over the Cuckoos Nest* by Ken Kesey. The professor's interpretation of Kesey's book was a marvelous exposition of the resurrection as stepping out of the boat. Sometimes we wonder if the author of a book has in mind all of the hidden meanings other people find when reading the book. The professor said that after Kesey had written the first draft he gave it to a friend. When the friend returned the book, he pointed out to Kesey that the character of McMurphy was a Christ figure. Kesey went back to work and in the final draft made the Christological aspect more pronounced.

By this time the members of the Coos Bay church knew that when I had been at a conference or on a study leave I would present what I had received. Usually the ideas were quite different from traditional theology. In this case I gave them a chance to prepare for what I would say and urged them to read Kesey's book because a sermon would follow. This is that sermon:

"*One Flew Over the Cuckoos Nest* is set in the ward of a mental hospital. McMurphy comes into the most orderly and well-run ward in the hospital. When he walks through the door, things begin to happen. He shakes hands with everyone, laughing and joking all the time. Laughter is something new on that ward. Not only have the men forgotten how to laugh, they are very ill at ease with all of McMurphy's joking and laughing. First he shakes hands with the Acutes, the ones the doctors figure can be cured. Then he shakes hands with the Chronics, the people who are in this world with flaws that defy repair.

"McMurphy is a clown, a gambler and a manipulator. He loves life and lives it to its fullest, and this brings him into conflict with the establishment. He is also a 'take-charge' person. When such a person arrives on a ward that is run with precision, orderliness, and no departure from that orderliness, conflict is on the way. Soon a battle of wits between McMurphy and the Big Nurse is in full swing and you find yourself rooting for McMurphy. Once in a while the rules get to him, but usually when this happens he regains control of himself and sees how funny the whole situation is. He can laugh at the rules, the disapproving looks of the Big Nurse, and being talked to as if he and rest of the men were three-year-olds. His laughter and disregard for the stupid rules aggravates the Big Nurse. McMurphy is safe as long as he can laugh, and this works most of the time.

"For instance, during a weekly ward meeting, the Big Nurse outwits McMurphy and defeats his intention of changing the television time so they can watch the world series. When it comes time for the game McMurphy pulls up his chair before the television set and flicks it on. When the picture appears, the Big Nurse flicks a switch and the picture is gone. McMurphy just sits there watching. Soon he is joined by the other men in the ward. They are all lined up in front of a black television set just as if they could see the ball game clearly. Big Nurse rants and screams at them, to no avail. If anyone had looked in on that scene they would have thought the whole bunch were as crazy as loons.

"Later in the story McMurphy has a change of heart. He discovers the rest of the men can leave the hospital anytime they wish. He has been committed, and the length of his stay will be determined by the Big Nurse. He decides to play it safe and follow the rules. The men on the ward do not understand this changed attitude. They were finally getting enough courage of their own to buck the system, and now all of a sudden their champion is not giving them any support. One day the Big Nurse's attitude toward something the men have done gets to McMurphy and the battle resumes.

"In the beginning of the third section, McMurphy has gained the upper hand over the Big Nurse and is running the show. He succeeds in setting up a fishing trip for some of the Acutes and Chief Broom. In the middle of this trip the men are liberated from the prison of themselves and become free. They have caught a big fish, and in the excitement of everyone helping to land the fish, McMurphy stands above them laughing. He is laughing at the whole world, and soon everyone on the boat has joined McMurphy in the laughter. There stands McMurphy surrounded by his dozen men. There are twelve plus McMurphy.

"This is a picture of salvation. These human beings are free. They are laughing themselves silly and in their laughter is freedom, because McMurphy knows that you have to laugh at the things that hurt you to keep yourself in balance. You have to laugh at the world to keep from making yourself plumb crazy. Yes, there is a painful side, but you do not let the pain blot out the humor any more than you let the humor blot out the pain.

"When the men return to the ward, they exercise their new freedom which creates more conflict. Trying to carry out ward policy one of the ward boys (hospital staff) goes too far and provokes Chief Broom into a fight. The other two ward boys come to help out, and McMurphy comes to the aid of Chief Broom. McMurphy and Chief Broom lose the fight and are taken upstairs to a place known as 'Disturbed,' where they are to receive electrical shock. When it comes to their turn, McMurphy insists on going first. He assures Chief Broom that they cannot hurt him, and therefore, they cannot hurt Chief Broom. Here is the Christ figure. McMurphy goes ahead of Chief Broom. Not only does he go first, he gets up on the table and spreads his arms out in the form of a cross.

"In this action you have death and resurrection taking place. This experience is the beginning of a new life for Chief Broom. When they return to the ward the battle of wits continues, but now it is carried on by all of the men. Feeling secure, they plan a big party for one evening. They intend to clean up their mess before the Big Nurse comes to work in the morning, but it does not happen. The party lasts too long. The men do not wake up in the morning. When the Big Nurse walks in and sees the mess she loses her cool. This leads to a final confrontation. McMurphy starts after her, but she runs for the safety of her station. Again McMurphy loses the battle and ends up on 'Disturbed.' This time he gets a lobotomy. He returns to the ward a 'vegetable.'

"Are we victims of our environment? Are we at the mercy of all the forces that seem to control our lives? How much strain and effort do we put into breaking out of the boxes which society has imposed on us? The story is set in a psychiatric ward because the world in which we live is just that crazy. To put it in New Testament language, we live in a demonic world that is just as crazy as a psychiatric ward. McMurphy is committed to the ward. We are committed to this world, and we cannot get out of it. The question we all have to answer is 'How will we live our lives?' We can play it safe. We can observe all the laws and live up to the conventions of society. If we do, society will like us. We may get some peace and harmony but we will be dehumanizing ourselves. Or, like McMurphy, we can break laws. Remember Jesus broke laws – those laws which would dehumanize human beings. He broke those laws which sought to bind people into neat little religious boxes, and in doing this Jesus sought to bring us to know and to live the fullness of our humanity."

After the experience with *One Flew Over the Cuckoos Nest*, I expanded the idea of looking for the Christian message to include movies, plays and television programs. *Who's Afraid of Virginia Wolfe?* was going to be in the Coos Bay area. With some of the other ministers, my congregation and I planned an evening to watch the movie followed by small discussion groups throughout the area. I remember watching the people as they left the movie theater. They were silent. There was none of the usual talking or laughter which follows most movies. I wondered what the silence meant.

People did not want to talk. Discussion proved to be very difficult, and after a short time I closed the meeting. Thinking about that experience I realized the subject matter was too close to home for them to discuss. I decided to be more careful about the kind of movie I would use for discussion. The next Sunday in the coffee hour someone said to me, "You know, I cannot even watch a television program without thinking theologically." "Good," I thought to myself, "That is what you ought to do."

By this time "getting out of the boat" was becoming more than just a phrase. It meant we had not been delivered out of the world but into it. We had to face all of the risks involved in living in this world. It might have appeared that in getting out of the boat we had been left to sink or swim. Not quite. There was help. We had not been left on our own. We did have the teachings of Jesus in the Sermon on the Mount and in the parables. Our journey had exposed us to new ideas and they became the help we needed. Underlying all of them was the idea behind the Greek word "agape" translated by the English word, love. If we understood "agape" then we could face the chaotic world in which we live. I decided it was time to explain the connection to the congregation:

"I hear people say, 'I love my dog, my car, my home, my new dress, my wife, my children,' and I wonder, 'Is there no difference?' When we give such a litany of things we 'love,' we are equating 'liking' with 'loving.' From the Biblical point of view these are not the same. In the New Testament the writers had a problem when they wanted to talk about what they understood Yahweh had done in Jesus, the Christ. In the Greek language there were several words which they could have used. There was 'phileo' a word expressing deep emotional feeling towards others. There was 'Eros,' an intense word associated with the physical, emotional and sexual desire. There were others they would not even consider. None fit the bill. They needed a new word.

"Because no common word was adequate, they invented the word 'agape.' Agape is a word that does not express being filled with emotion or feeling, but rather is an act of a person's will. Many theologians have reminded us that Christian love is not primarily an emotion or an affection; it is an active determination of our wills. This is why it can be commanded, as feelings cannot. Loving and liking are not the same. Romantic love, friendship, and genuine affection are feelings which we cannot turn on and off like water from a faucet. But kindness, generosity, mercy, patience, concern, righteous indignation are dispositions of our will. They are attitudes which we can make ourselves embrace. They are possible directions in which our actions can go out toward others, regardless of our feelings. 'Agape' wills our neighbor's good whether we like him or not! Jesus put it in these terms: 'Love your enemies and pray for your persecutors. . . if you only love those who love you, what reward can you expect?. . . Even the heathen do as much.' (1)

"A woman who had spent most of her life doing social work in Chicago was being interviewed. Asked if she liked her work she responded in the negative. She did not like the conditions in which those people had to live and work even when they found work. She did not like the filth, the hopelessness, the discrimination, or many of the people she was required to help. Finally the interviewer asked, 'Why did you continue if you did not like what you were doing?' She replied, 'Because as a Christian I must love them.' Agape wills the neighbor's good whether we like the neighbor or not. This 'love' reaches out to others, and does so, not because we are emotional, but because it is our duty.

"In the Gospel of Matthew we read, 'Love the Lord your God with all you heart, mind, and soul, . . . and your neighbor as yourself.' (2) 'Agape' takes us beyond our feelings to meet the needs of others.

"'Who is my neighbor?' someone asked Jesus. His reply shocked his hearers. He told about a traveler being accosted by thieves, stripped, beaten, and left to die. Without any clothes on him, the man's social status was unknown. The people who heard this parable fully expected that after the Priest and the Levite refused to stop and help the man, the hero would be a faithful Israelite. Instead, it was a half-breed, a heretic, a Samaritan.

"In modern terms, the story goes this way. A man was on his way to attend church when he ran out of gas. He cussed his shortsightedness for not having checked the gas gauge. Being on a freeway, he lifted the hood of his car and expected a quick ride. No such luck. Many cars passed him, filled with good church-going people. None stopped to give a helping hand. Too risky. As he was about to give up a car stopped. A black man got out of his car and asked what the trouble was. When the white man told him, the black man offered to take him to the nearest gas station. The white man accepted. They drove to the nearest exit which indicated there was a gas station. They filled a gas can and returned to the white man's car. The black man helped put the gas in the tank and made sure the white man was on his way. The black man, an advocate of black power, continued on his journey. He was on his way to lead a demonstration. That is the kind of twist found in the parable of the good Samaritan. 'Agape' does not ask 'Who is my neighbor?'

"In reaching out to meet the needs of others 'agape' does not try to make them over into our kind of person. 'Agape' does not reach out to usurp the rights of the other. Romantic love chooses its object. Christian love does not. To 'love' in the Christian sense means we can no longer use the excuse, 'After all, I am only human.' When we say that, we are simply making an excuse for not taking our responsibility in a difficult situation. In the sixties there was a man who did get out of the boat, and he confronted the dehumanizing forces in his life. He did not use the excuse 'After all, I am only human.' Martin Luther King Jr. took the risks involved in leading his people in demanding racial equality. He confronted the issues of race with nonviolence.

"On his marches and demonstrations, he accomplished more than all the pious prayers of hundreds of thousands of white Christians praying for the unity of humankind, hoping that God would take care of the matter when they left the sanctuary. In the resurrection we are not called to pray, but to get out of the boat and, with 'agape' in our hearts, wrestle with the chaotic forces of this world. No longer can we use the excuse, 'After all, I am only human.'"

For me, one meaning of getting out of the boat, was the growing conviction I had to confront the institutional church for failing to have even considered the gauntlet thrown down by the no-God theologians. Somewhere, somehow, I wanted the Presbyterian church to talk about the doctrine of "God." My opportunity came when I attended a committee meeting to plan some workshops on worship.

The chairman, a minister, opened the meeting with prayer. That was standard procedure. Whenever Presbyterians get together we pray before we begin our business, in the middle of the meeting, and certainly before we leave. When the minister had finished his opening prayer, I asked, "Why did you open the meeting with prayer?" This took him by surprise. He replied, "To make sure God was present in the meeting to give us guidance." I responded, "What would you do if God decided not to come to our meeting? Would that invalidate what we are about to do? Is it possible we could do our business without being religious? Does the mouthing of some words we call prayer make our meeting legal from God's point of view?"

After a pause I asked, "What is your definition of God?" He replied, "God is omnipresence, omnipotent, and immutable," and that ended the discussion. He did not allow it to continue. I held my tongue, listened to a lot of tripe and finally suggested that, if God was up there, Almighty and All-powerful, I could not understand why we were meeting. The form of worship for most Presbyterians already fits that concept of God. Making worship a bit more formal was not a step forward.

The Presbyterian church had just issued a new *Book of Common Worship Provisional Services*. The national committee working on revisions had removed the "Thees" and "Thous" and changed the order of worship, making it less formal. From my point of view, discarding the "Thees" and "Thous" was not enough. The concept of the God-up-there had not been changed. The prayers were the same. If we, as a committee on worship, were going to do anything about worship, we really needed to address the issue of God-talk. I had not won that argument.

Returning to Coos Bay, I shifted our attention to another matter. The theological discussion of the no-God theologians had also produced a discussion about so-called situational ethics. The ideas in situational ethics went hand in hand with "agape." It really is the basis for the Christian's moral decisions. We need to ask the question:

"How does any one make an ethical decision? Some people are armed with rules and regulations immutable, unchangeable, holy, and not to be tampered with. If a person flaunts or breaks them, they are in deep trouble. The key words in this approach are 'always' and 'never.' When faced with making a moral decision they just whip out the book of authority and flip through its pages until they find an answer. The shortcoming of this approach is assigning absolute validity to the rules or laws and not having any leeway in applying them. This was the approach of the Pharisees in Jesus' day, and is the approach of the institutional churches and television evangelists in our time.

"The basis for this comes from the account of Moses going to the top of Mount Sinai where he spent a long time chipping away on some tablets of stone. He returned with what are known as the Ten Commandments. Right? Wrong! What Moses received were the teachings of Yahweh. Simply put, Yahweh said, 'This is how you are to live in relationship to each other. If you follow these teachings, you will find life. If you do not, then you are asking for trouble. These teachings are the danger zones in human lives. If you decide to tread in the danger zones, be ready for the consequences. The choice is up to you.' It is really that simple. What Moses received were the teachings of Yahweh for living human life. They were not commands. Commands are orders given in the military which, when you break them, lead to court martial. It is unfortunate that we made the switch from 'the teachings' to 'the commandments.'

"A different approach within the context of the Christian faith that gained some acceptance in the sixties was called 'The New Morality,' or 'Situational Ethics.' When I heard of these 'new ethics,' I did not feel anything was new. The New Morality was restating what had always been true for most Christians. 'Situational Ethics' promoted the idea that in any given situation you had principles which helped you make a decision. There were no hard, fast, binding rules. The rules were guidelines. They were wise sayings from the experiences of the past to help us get the essence of 'agape' into our actions. When we are in a situation where none of the past principles clearly gives us help – you know, those gray areas of living where most decisions have to be made – then we must make our own decision on how to respond.

"Situational ethics says there is a shift from laws and commandments to person-centered decisions. The basis of morality is to 'love' people and use things, not love things and use people. Principles, being statements, can be used against people. If we insist on using the word commandment, then we should put the words 'usually' or 'ordinarily' or 'in most cases' after each of them. But in reality when we take the 'Teachings of Yahweh' and turn them into immutable laws called the ten commandments, we have become immoral.

"A professor, known for his advocacy of situational ethics, was returning from a conference. Sitting next to him on the airplane was a beautiful young woman. During their conversation she discovered he was a professor of ethics and asked him for his advice. She had been approached by the CIA to become an agent. She emphasized that if she did she would have to compromise her sexual ethics. Finally she asked him if she should accept the job.

His reply, 'No.'

" 'Why?' she asked.

" 'You talk too much,' he replied.

"In reality most of us are situationalists in making moral decisions. We do have moral teachings we carry with us. If we find ourselves in a situation where we might have to bend them somewhat because we are in one of the gray areas of life with no definite rule to guide us, we no longer need to feel guilty if we stretch our guidelines a bit. Most of us have been doing that all of our lives. It has been said, 'If we love (agape) then we can do as we please.' That is true. Situational ethics is the 'love' ethic finding 'love's' relative course in any given situation."

An honest preacher always finds his words reflecting back onto his own life and actions. This approach to making ethical decisions had an affect on my sexual activities. If I had sought sex with another woman, I would have felt I was being unfaithful. By this time I had decided that I was not bisexual; I was gay. This was finding the relative course in my sexuality. Since I was gay, if I was approached by another man, or found myself in the presence of a man who indicated he was gay and there was an attraction between us which we carried out, I felt I was handling my sexuality in a responsible manner. I did not feel I was being unfaithful when I was with a man. Remember, this was an agreement my wife and I had made some years before.

Finally it dawned on me that I was not looking just for sex, but some man I could love. Deep within I began to know that I wanted one man with whom I could be intimate – mentally, spiritually and physically. If I did meet Mr. Wonderful I would have to be faithful to him. If I had been straight I would have remained faithful to my wife.

I often thought of King David, Israel's great king in the Old Testament. He had a couple of wives, a love affair with Jonathan, and possible incestuous thoughts about one of his sons. Despite all of this, he was the model of what a King of Israel should be. Looking for an answer to my situation, I felt a relationship with another minister might just be the answer. We could have an affair and still appear to be straight to the world. A relationship would enable me to handle my whole life in a positive and constructive manner. That is what I thought.

One day at a meeting of Presbytery it happened. There was Mr. Wonderful. He was my physical type, what I considered very attractive. I hoped he was my "type" in every way. I decided to become acquainted. He was an assistant minister, and I had empathy for ministers who were working as assistants. Having served in that capacity I knew the frustrations he would face. As ministers we had not been trained to work in a staff situation. One of my professors in seminary, when talking about a staff position, would always say, "It is better to be the head of a mouse, than the tail of a rat." Needless to say, this did not encourage anyone to consider a staff position. Yet it had always seemed to me that ministers, of all people, should be able to work as a team.

Naturally I spent as much time with Mr. Wonderful as possible whenever we attended the same meetings. We shared some of the same ideas concerning the issues before the Presbyterian church. He seemed to enjoy my company. We attended a two-day conference. I sat next to him, and every now and then, I thought I was getting signals indicating he was interested in more than just a friendship. They were the same signals gay men used when trying to meet each other in any straight situation. That evening several of us gathered in his room. I waited until the others had left and we were alone. I had decided to follow through on the given signals and take the risk of telling him I was gay and interested in him. If he was not gay, I hoped I could trust him. With fear and trembling, my voice uncertain, a knot in my stomach, I told him how I felt. I had not misinterpreted his signals! He had been giving them to me throughout the day. He said he was not gay. He had been to a conference on homosexuality, had learned about the signals gay men give to each other and wanted to see if they worked. "Thanks a whole bunch." I thought. "They had worked all right."

I felt this was a bit underhanded, but said nothing. A tinge of fear began to settle in the pit of my stomach. "Would he keep that knowledge to himself?" I hoped he would. I also hoped we would remain friends. But that tinge of fear never quite left.

A few months after that encounter in Mr. Wonderful's room, the phone rang on a Sunday afternoon. The caller asked me to meet him and some other ministers at the church. He did not state the reason for their visit. He did not have to. I knew why they had come. As a gay man living in the closet, I lived in constant fear of being found out. Every day was lived in the fear of this happening. When I arrived at the church I was met by the moderator of the Presbytery, the chairman of the Ministerial Relations Committee, and the Synod Executive. That was one powerful group of ministers to visit another minister on a Sunday afternoon. It was like a Catholic priest in some forgotten, obscure town being visited by his bishop and the Pope! I was impressed. I was also very nervous and scared to death.

They told me Mr. Wonderful had talked with them at the last meeting of the Presbytery. He had noticed my leaving the meeting more than necessary. Knowing I was a homosexual, he was sure I had been leaving the meeting to go cruising for a sexual partner.

This information floored me. He had not come to me any time during the meeting, or after, to find out if his assumptions were true. Some friend! Mr. Wonderful had become the Rev. Mr. Judas. Fortunately my psychiatrist had prepared me for this kind of situation. He told me that if this happened, I should tell them my sexual life was my affair, and they did not need to know about it. That was only partially true. If the Presbytery had the goods on me, I could have been defrocked – drummed out of the ministry. The scandal would not have helped any of us.

When a Presbyterian congregation is without an installed pastor, a member of the Presbytery (usually another minister) is assigned to be the moderator of the Session. The Session is the ruling body of a local Presbyterian church and the installed pastor is the moderator of the Session. The moderator functions as does the president of any organization. I told my visitors I was moderator of the Bandon Presbyterian Church and I had been making phone calls trying to find a minister to preach at the Bandon church the Sunday following the meeting of Presbytery. That answer satisfied them. But they were also concerned about my wife. I told them she was aware of the situation and both of us were seeing a psychiatrist. We had my being gay under control. If they wanted, they were free to call the psychiatrist. If my memory serves me correctly, I think they did and accepted his assessment of our situation. To the credit of those ministers, the issue was closed. They kept the knowledge to themselves. That ended that, at least for the time being. I was becoming aware that there were pitfalls in being a gay minister.

I thought about the Rev. Mr. Judas, and in the back of my mind flashed the thought, "There is a Judas in every person's' life." Following this episode it began to dawn on me that being gay was not a choice, it was a given. It was the bad experiences more than the good ones which convinced me of this. No person in his right mind, and I was in my right mind, would choose a lifestyle filled

95

with that kind of danger when he had a good wife and family.

About this time three gay men moved to Coos Bay. They worked in a steak house. In the latter part of the afternoon I would go to the restaurant. It became a place where gays in that small town could get together in relative safety. Here I could be myself. I did not have to be constantly on guard fearing I might slip in something I said or did. Often there were no customers and the guys usually had their work finished and had time to sit and talk. For me it was a time to be with gay friends. Unless you are part of a despised group of people, you do not know what a relief it is to be among your own. This short time each day enabled me to handle the lie I was living in a more positive manner.

A little more than three years had passed since "That Sunday." It was time to reflect on what had taken place and what the future might be. We had been going in a new direction and had emphasized change. Our message was not based on a series of birthday celebrations at Christmastime commemorating the past, but rather on an understanding of the Easter event, signaling resurrection and hope for the future. Change did not come easily, and we did not change everything at one time. What changes had been made had come primarily from suggestions made by the members. Because we had the courage to "be change" in the total life of the congregation, some members of long-standing left. For me as a pastor, this was difficult to accept. The loss in membership was one of the real burdens of the journey. I should have known this would happen, but I did not want to accept it. It was a mixed blessing; new people were drawn to our church because we had dared to express new patters of theology in the worship and life of the congregation.

We were experimenting with different forms of worship. One service which stood out was the morning we had a reading of Camus' play "A Misunderstanding." Toward the end of the coffee hour when I announced the beginning of the Talk-Back, the room was filled. Most of the discussion was between the people. I listened. As a congregation we were becoming aware that our traditional order of worship did not fit our concept of God. We found that the words of many of the hymns were also at odds with our theological thinking.

At the end of the discussion I asked if anyone was interested in working with me on new forms of worship. I was convinced of the importance of worship in the life of the congregation, not as a religious exercise, but because it was one resource we had to prepare us to go out into the world to serve. No one volunteered. They were glad to leave it up to me.

What changes I made had to do with the words used in worship. For instance, the Prayer of Confession of Sin changed to "A Time for Looking Within." In the old confessional prayer we talked about how ashamed we were of all our sins, of having let our lower, selfish desires rule us, and then the minister gave us assurance that our sins had been forgiven. The only trouble with that was we had to return each week and confess all over again. In the Time for Looking Within we talked about being the body of Christ in this world, specifically in Coos Bay. In the presence of those in attendance we needed to consider what this meant. The members were urged to silently examine their own lives, and at the end I would say, "Therefore, if anyone is in Christ, they are a new person. Go into the world and live in 'love.'"

One way a minister gets a feeling of support from the congregation is attendance at worship. It is also an indication of the health of the church and its program. Our attendance had been declining since June of 1968. The financial status of any congregation is the second indication of the state of affairs and often follows attendance. But our financial situation had remained steady. I took comfort in the idea that since our money is an extension of ourselves, perhaps there is a great deal of truth to the saying – where your money is, there is your heart. I wanted to think the finances balanced the drop in attendance. There seemed to be a contradiction between the two. I shrugged my shoulders and wondered what it all meant.

One positive note was the increase in the number of adult study groups. People in the study groups were aware that lurking in the back of my mind was the need for the institutional church to rewrite the gospels for our time. I was waiting for some great scholar to do this, not me. Many of us had been taught that once The Bible had been written that was that. Yahweh had stopped speaking. The institutional churches insisted their creeds said everything that needed to be said. But that was an idea I never really accepted. Now I knew that Yahweh had continued to speak throughout the ages. The new ideas concerning who Jesus was, and is, convinced me that Yahweh was speaking once again through the work of scholars.

Another milestone took place between my wife and myself. I came home one afternoon unexpectedly and found her looking out of the living room window, just staring, not moving, not responding to my arrival. I did not blame her. If only I could have been able to go and put my arms around her and comfort her. But I could not do that. Perhaps you have noticed that I have not mentioned my wife's name. The omission is not accidental. All through our married life I could not call her by her name. If I wanted to talk with her I went to wherever she was. I had noticed that other men, when talking about their wives in a group, would use their wives' names. Not me, I always said, 'my wife.' There was always that distance. No wonder I could not physically go to her aid at this time.

As I thought about that afternoon I felt it would help her if she had something more meaningful to do. We had had a division of labor. I did the work outside the house and she took care of the inside tasks. She was an excellent seamstress and enjoyed knitting. But she needed something more, something that would give some purpose to her life other than everyday work and staring out the window.

A few days later I suggested she go back to work. The children were old enough and did not need her at home all of the time. She had been a secretary before our marriage, and her experience would help her now. She did return to work. She was the only person in the office who did not have to rush home and get dinner prepared. She had planned the meal and the children were responsible to prepare it.

In a short time she made her presence known in the office. She did not bow down when the President of the college came into the secretary's office. In fact she would stand up to him, which none of the other workers would do. In a short time she became the executive secretary to the president of the community college, and she ran the president as most good secretaries run their bosses. Her secretarial skills had come to our rescue.

With the added income we decided to invest in some property. We purchased about forty-eight acres on the West Fork of the Allegheny river in the coastal mountains. We called it "The Ranch." Not very original, but for someone who had been raised in Wisconsin, this piece of land qualified as a ranch.

It was a beautiful piece of property with a county road running through the middle of it. Entering the property was not impressive; the hills on both sides rose rather steeply, blocking any view. Soon, however, a small stream ran under the road, and the road widened, not much, but enough so that on the left was a small house, and to the right a trail large enough for a car or pickup. The road clung to the side of a hill for a short distance more, and then it entered a large, grassy meadow bounded by a rushing stream on the left, and the beautiful Allegheny river at the end.

Just before you arrived at the meadow there was a barn, in the middle of a neglected apple orchard. The property had been a farm in past years, but no one had worked it for a long time. In the winter you could watch the steelhead swim up the stream to spawn. Toward the bottom of the meadow was a small stand of Christmas trees. At Christmas time the kids and I could look in our own little grove for our Christmas tree. We always made sure we found one with a bird's nest, as we had been given a family of birds as Christmas decorations. We created some wonderful memories in our tree searches.

Since the house was not usable, the meadow became our own park for summer activities with Robert R.'s family, the adopted grandparents and one or two other families. This was the basis of our social life. Having time alone with my wife was not a high priority and I used times with this small group of people as a substitute for taking my wife out for an evening together. I remember the first Fourth of July our extended family enjoyed in the meadow. I soon had a campfire going. Some of the kids were throwing Frisbees with one or two parents while others played horseshoes, and the older people sat under the apples trees enjoying the kids, the quiet and each other. This was the first of many picnics this group of people enjoyed.

The ranch became a refuge for me to get away from everything and everyone. The meadow was a gardener's heaven. Here I had all the space I wanted for a garden and I could raise the hot weather plants – tomatoes, corn, melons – which were difficult to grow in Coos Bay which was so close to the ocean. At least that is what I thought. With hammer, saw, nails, chicken wire, and a few other tools I decided to put a fence around the garden. I needed to protect the tomatoes and other plants from the deer, elk, and perhaps bears. There were plenty of scattered two-by-fours around the barn to build the fence. Soon it was finished, and I planted the tomatoes, corn and melons which would ripen the middle of September.

Throughout the summer the plants grew as they should, except the melons. This puzzled me, until one day it dawned on me that, even though the days were hot, the evenings cooled down. Melons like warm nights as much or more than warm days. Oh, well, I had the rest of the garden. September arrived, and on the first Sunday when I woke up and opened the drapes I could not believe my eyes. I rubbed them, looked again. I was not dreaming. I was seeing frost all over the outside. This just was not possible; frost did not hit Oregon this early. But it had. There it was. Being an optimist I crossed my fingers as I went out to the ranch as soon as possible. My worst fears came true. The garden had been killed by the frost. I was not the only person whose garden had suffered. The frost covered the whole state. More interesting is that such an early frost has not hit Oregon since.

That old phrase that the best laid plans of men and mice do go astray brought home to me our struggle as human beings on this earth. Our journey had explored the doctrine of God, shifted to who Jesus was and is, but now it was time to consider the role of human beings. My next teachings can be summed up with a look at the myth of Adam and Eve.

"One of the most fantastic passages in the Bible is the second chapter of Genesis. This is the Biblical account of the beginning of the human race. The writer says that Yahweh took the dust of the earth and breathed into his nostrils a breath of life,' and the man became a living being. (The Hebrew word 'adam' means the human race, not an individual man) Fantastic! When the 'breath' of Yahweh permeated that body, we became human beings. It is this 'breath' which separates us from the animal world. We are freed from being programmed into a particular manner of life, and responding in a set way to any given situation. We do not live only by instinct. We became persons. Not just the highest killer primate.

"Yahweh created a wonderful garden in which to live. 'Everything in this garden is for your use,' said Yahweh. 'Enjoy it. Oh, by the way, see that tree over there? Well, you cannot eat the fruit it produces.' There was no guardian angel protecting the tree, no electric fence around it. It just stood there like all of the other trees. Well, you know what happened. In the creation of human beings, Yahweh took a fantastic chance. We were given real freedom. That meant we could make wrong choices, set the wrong direction in our lives, have the wrong value systems.

"The first response of Adam and Eve, when tempted, was to eat the forbidden fruit. After they did, there was no lightening, no immediate judgment. But that evening, when it was time to walk with Yahweh in the garden, Adam and Eve hid. They were ashamed. They felt guilty. The punishment, the consequence of their misuse of freedom was experienced within and not from some outside power.

"We are dealing with myth. This means we can get beyond the 'how it happened,' and concentrate on the meaning of the myth. Myths are one method of unfolding the meaning of our humanness. One important truth from the account is that the world in which we live is not heaven. Our lives were not meant to be an eternal life time spent in Disneyland, or on the beach, or skiing in the mountains. Our life on this earth is the creative tension between the 'soul' within us – our potential – and the 'flesh,' the desire to live only on the physical. Our task in our lifetime is to take both sides and create a unity.

"Our job is to balance these two forces within us. It is Yahweh's breath which enables us to break the evolutionary past. We are more than our instincts. We have a soul which means we can control our emotions, our instincts. The implantation of Yahweh's breath gave us a potential beyond that of any other creature. How great? Jesus said, 'Love your enemies and pray for your persecutors, only so can you be children of your heavenly Father, who makes his sun rise on good and bad alike, and sends the rains on the honest and dishonest. If you love those who love you, what reward can you expect? . . . Even the heathen do as much. You must therefore be all goodness, just as your heavenly father is all good.' (3) In the death and resurrection of Jesus, the Christ, these two powerful forces, which are within everyone's life, came to blows. The crucifixion – aggression at its worst – was not the end. 'Agape' – Easter – won the battle. The message of the New Testament is – this 'love' can reside within each of us."

As a human being struggling with both the aggressive and "love" aspects, I was most aggressive when involved with theological concepts. The journey which we had taken in Coos Bay needed to be shared with other congregations. These theological ideas were important not just for the congregation at Coos Bay. As a member of Presbyter's Committee on Christian Education I urged the committee to set up a workshop to consider some of the ideas of the No-God theologians. The workshop was divided into two sections. One would introduce church school teachers to Inductive Teaching, and I would have a chance to stretch their minds in the realm of theology. I was given three hours (with a break, of course) to explore the theological concepts found *One Flew Over the Cuckoos Nest*. In the notices announcing this worship, we urged people to read the book before they came.

When I arrived in Klamath Falls where the workshop was to be held, I was met by the pastor of the local Presbyterian Church, who immediately took me off for a cup of coffee. My guard went up because most of the time we never saw pastors at our educational workshops, so being invited by the host pastor for coffee was very unusual. We chit-chatted for a few moments before he got to the point. He did not want me to talk about Kesey's book. That really floored me. He had been in the same seminar with me. "So, what's the big deal?" I asked. He replied, "I do not accept the ideas given and have forbidden my members to read the book." I could not believe my ears.

"You what? Told your members they could not read the book?"

"Yes," he said. "After I had read your announcement I told my members not to read the book."

I was stunned and for a moment speechless. When I recovered I said, "You certainly do not have to accept this interpretation of Kesey's book, but I do not think your position as pastor allows you to censor what your people read." I assured him I was not going to say anything he had not heard in the seminar. This did not change his mind. I did not change what I had prepared.

As I discussed Kesey's book, I also attacked many of the traditional concepts of the Christian faith which I had questioned during the past several years. In the discussion period a woman asked, "Are you a Christian?" I replied, "From your perspective probably not. But as I understand the New Testament I can say, 'Yes.'" A little later in the discussion someone asked me if I ever went to God in prayer for an answer to a specific situation or problem which I faced. I replied, "No. The will of God is not unknown. It is found throughout the Bible. All we have to do is live it. It is really that simple."

Later in the day the report came back to me that my answer had prompted one of the ministers to say, "That is the height of egotism on the part of that man." Not really, the Bible is our guideline on how to live our lives by the "Will of God."

It is the institutional church which keeps people thinking the "Will of God" is some mysterious knowledge we must somehow or other wrestle out of God so we can know what to do. No way! It's all there. Look at the Sermon On The Mount in the Gospel of Matthew. It is a guide for how to live when we get out of the boat and have to face the terrors and risks of living in this world. It is not easy to live by the teachings of Jesus. There is a risk involved. That is freedom. That is what most of us do not want to do. We prefer to have a God-up-there whom we can beseech to tell us what to do in situations where the answer is not clear. We really prefer not having to take the responsibility for our decisions and actions. To me, having to make difficult decisions in the gray areas of life is what is difficult about being human. It is not whether the decision is right or wrong, but that we made a decision and are willing to live with the consequences.

Some time later, I was in my office pondering the need to reexamine the history of the church and its roots in various cultures rather than just Palestine. A knock on my office door interrupted my thoughts. Looking up I saw a young man standing there. "Come in, have a seat," I said. After the usual pleasantries he said, "I want to apply for a conscientious objector status with the draft board, and I would appreciate it if you would write a letter to that affect." He named some people in the community who had suggested he come and talk with me. He admitted his relationship with the Coos Bay Presbyterian Church had not been much in the past. No surprise. I did not recognize him or his family name as being connected with the membership of the church. Being a member was not a requirement to receive help.

We talked about the reasons behind his wanting a conscientious objector status. During the conversation I came to believe he was sincere. His objection to military service was based on his belief in "God." He also promised he would become more involved in the life of the church. I told him I would write to the draft board supporting his request. Not long after this interview, I received a letter from the draft board informing me they had granted his request. That visit was the first and last time I saw him. "Well, so much for that."

A week later another knock on my door. Another young man stood in the doorway. The young man's attire indicated he was a "hippie." I invited him in and a long discussion followed. We talked about human life, human values and a person's responsibility to society and his fellow human beings. Not once in our conversation did he mention the word "God." Yet all the time we talked, I felt we had been talking about the meaning of "God." I had the feeling we were on the same wave length. Here was a young man living his faith not just talking about it. My letter to the draft board on his behalf was to no avail. They sent me a letter telling me so. Why? I can only guess. But I had a sneaking suspicion that since the young man did not believe in the God-up-there, they would not grant his request. His deep concern and love for his fellow human beings was not acceptable to the draft board. When I had finished reading their letter I thought to myself, "What would they do with me? I do not believe in a God-up-there, and I am an ordained, practicing Presbyterian minister." Certainly the draft board was playing 'God,' only I did not think they thought they were.

In 1969 I had a wonderful experience. I was a commissioner to the General Assembly meeting of the United Presbyterian Church. For most ministers this is a once in a lifetime experience. It was an exciting meeting. The race issue was graphically thrust before us in the presence of James Forman who demanded retributions be paid to black people for the damage white churches had done to blacks. That caused great concern among the delegates who were unsure what to do. I remember the pleas of the black Presbyterian ministers that we seriously consider the impact of Forman's challenge. Their pleas were heard. The General Assembly did not give Forman any money, but programs were developed to give help. In the ensuing marches and demonstrations for racial equality many Presbyterians were in the middle of things.

Following the meeting I went to visit my parents. On the way I decided to visit Brad. It had been a long time since my last visit, and this stop would not be out of my way. The closer I got, the greater my anxiety. I wondered how I would feel about him and he about me. We had not kept in close touch through the years, and this made my actions more difficult. I walked up to the door of his house, paused, and finally rang the bell. The door opened, and there he was. All of my feelings were still there. I still loved him. His welcome was warm and friendly. We picked up where we had left off since our last time together. Later that day his wife sent us to the grocery store. On the way I told him that I had loved him all of these years. He replied that he had known that. I gave him a hug. He returned it. The visit was wonderful. I left and went to my parents. Brad is still part of my life deep within where memories are kept.

In the summer of 1969 the first American reached the moon. Although I was as amazed and excited as anyone about the fantastic physical accomplishment we as a nation had made, I also had some questions about the whole affair running around in my mind. Naturally I let the congregation know my thoughts.

"Why have we gone to the moon? What do we expect to accomplish? One answer, I suppose, is that we need to restore our national prestige and beat the Russians. Certainly the scientific community hopes to gain knowledge of the universe. But many people suspect the purpose was to develop military bases and reap the benefits of technology.
"From the Christian tradition these reasons were not enough. The accomplishment did reaffirm our self-image as Americans. A dream had come true. But it also allowed us

to forget, or at least set aside, our difficulty in Vietnam, the problems in our cities, the revolt of the young people and the race issue. The Biblical faith is not against our being in space. But the same technological know-how which carried Apollo II to the moon is threatening to destroy the very environment in which we must live. Humankind was given dominion over the earth to subdue it, to use, but not in the way we have done. We were not given license to rape, to destroy, to utterly devastate the earth.

"Since we have so fouled our air, land and water, will space be the only place left where we can live? We cannot continually run away from the problems we have created on earth. The Biblical faith says we are responsible for our actions, and if we misuse the things of this world, we will be confronted with the consequences. This was why many important people felt exhilaration in our going to the moon, but at the same time were disturbed and filled with despair. As Apollo II raced to the moon, many people besides myself thought of our dismal failure to solve our other problems – Vietnam, the ghettos in our cities, the quality of the natural environment, the unrest on the campuses.

"The decision to go to the moon was made, and we got there. The real issue was whether or not we, the people, would say to our government, 'No more. We do not need any further space exploration.' Only a few voices were raised in protest. Voices who were concerned with the problems of this world. For many people the great increase in violence, the unrest on the campuses, the breakdown of law and order, and overpopulation were at the top of the list. What will be the consequences if we do not control these things that seem so out of control?

"A psychologist conducted some experiments on a species of rats in Norway. The creatures had a clearly defined and attractive life style. They were hunters, but did not attack their own kind. They were monogamous with a clear mating ritual. The male pursued the female who escaped into her burrow. Then she put her head out to watch him dancing before her. Finally she emerged for the act of procreation. In the experiment, the size of the space available to the rats was significantly reduced. The results were astonishing. Some of the rats became apathetic, abandoning the hunt. Some became cruel, torturing their prey or even attacking their own kind. The whole mating ritual was destroyed. The males pursued the females into the borrows. Other disorders also became quite prevalent.

"We are human beings, not rats. But we have a long history as primates, and we know what happens when we forget the spiritual aspect of our lives. Or do we? We do not know what will happen as the amount of space for human life continues to shrink. In the history of our country, when neighbors came too close for comfort, we picked up stakes and went West. We cannot do that anymore. We have reached the end. Do we plan to run off to the moon or some other planet and thereby solve the problem of over-population? Most people in positions of authority do not think overpopulation is a major problem in 1969. But it is; we simply do not want to recognize it.

"If the Christian faith, or at least its by-product, Western culture, has looked with disdain at nature, then the Christian faith has not been true to the Biblical concept of creation. Or perhaps we never realized that as human beings we are co-creators with Yahweh. All of this world is here for our use, and when we have finished creating we ought to be able to say, 'And it was good.' The New Testament abounds in example after example which expresses our responsibility for our actions and our use of the things of this world.

"The term for one who is responsible is 'steward.' A steward is someone who has received something in trust, to be used as the owner wishes. The steward is responsible for how he or she uses it. If we misuse the things of this world we will not be hit by lightening. The pollution of this world is the judgment of our misuse. Do we have time to reverse the course of our misuse so that we will have a planet on which to live?" (Thirty years have passed since some of us expressed those ideas and only now are we beginning to understand that we must do something. The judgment of our misuse of this planet has come home to roost).

After some three years of destroying and trying to build something new at the church and in the community, I was beginning to feel very frustrated. It was like the summer my family and I were returning from a visit to my parents. We were in Eastern Washington headed to the Columbia river to cross over into Oregon. I had checked the road map for the highway which would take us out of Pasco, Washington and into Oregon. I did not notice which city in Oregon the highway would reach.

When we approached Pasco we were greeted with a new superhighway which bypassed Pasco and sent us off to who knew where. We came to an interchange, and I took what I thought was the correct turn. We came to a town but had not crossed the Columbia river. I turned around and headed back. I could not read the signs fast enough and, before I knew it, we were in another town and still had not crossed the river. My temper was beginning to assert itself and was not helped much by the smart aleck remarks from my family.

Before I lost my cool, I stopped at a gas station and asked for directions. Then it dawned on me. The number of the highway had been changed. In reality I had not been lost. I knew where I was going. I just did not know how to get there. I was hung up on the number of the old highway, the old symbol, the old sign. No one had told me it had been changed.

I felt this was the situation in the Coos Bay church. We were on a journey. The old signs and symbols had been discarded. No one had put up new ones. There were indications in the life of the congregation that added to the feeling of being really adrift. Attendance once again had taken a dip. This did not sit well with me. Only the women's organization was meeting as it had always done. We experimented with some new programs in the church school. The experts were telling us that parents should be involved with their children. Okay. Keeping in mind that a person learns by doing more than by listening, I came up with a program which started with a pot luck dinner and continued with a series of activities the children and their parents could do together leading them to the main theme for the evening. This sounded good in theory, but I discovered parents were not used to working with their children, and many of them more or less stood around.

I tried a new approach to our Senior High Program. Although they met each week, the emphasis was upon a retreat once a month. This program was more successful. It gave the young people and adults time to be with each other one-on-one or in small groups without pressure. They had time to explore Biblical themes and relate them to their daily lives. There was one young man who was an actor, not only at our retreats, but also in school, and he would keep us in stitches with his joking and humor. But none of these new programs could stem the loss in attendance on Sunday morning and the loss in membership.

Part of the problem was my one-track mind. So intent had I been on finding a new word for "God," that I did not realize my adventures into the meaning of the life of Jesus had been taking me in new directions. I had been waiting for the No-God theologians to come up with some answers. But they had not, probably because the news media reported their thinking before they had fully thought through their positions. Traditional theologians were defensive and argued with them. One well-known television evangelist blithely said, "God is not dead; I talked with Him this morning." When I heard that I said to myself, "Come on now, even you know better than to say that."

At least the Coos Bay Presbyterian Church had looked at some new ideas. We had learned the God-up-there, the God of the Caesars and the Napoleons was a creation of human beings and was not the "God" of the Scriptures. Our experience had shown that it was very difficult for new ideas of "god" to displace the old ones and become part of our lives. It would take time.

I did not feel totally lost. But I was not very sure of where we were. This lead to a sermon entitled, "Are we Lost?" The essence of that sermon was to explore whether or not I as their pastor was lost, and whether they as a congregation were lost. Their feeling of being lost had been expressed to me in such questions as, "What do I do when something happens to me? Do I return to the old answers we have left behind?"

I replied, " I cannot answer for you, but for me the answer is "No." To do so would be to return to the slavery of the theological ideas we have rejected Unfortunately I do not have a nice, neat, little package of new answers."

The next Sunday I said, "No, we are not lost," and pointed out there were some positive signs. We were beginning to understand the importance of those members who had not left. We did have each other. We were sharing the same difficulties, heartaches, troubles, joys, excitements and the wonders of our migration. We began to grow in understanding ourselves and our relationship to each other as a community of believers. Bonhoeffer's idea of the Christ being known only in the fellowship of believers was becoming a reality. We had discovered the value and sacredness of our human lives, which we share with all human beings. We had made some mistakes. But we had also grown.

The feeling of having grown came in worship. As we continued to plod along, we felt progress. Worship had changed to meet our needs and to express our understanding of the Christian life. Worship no longer consisted of sitting next to each other, enduring the service which celebrated the God-up-there, and waiting for it to end. Sunday mornings had become a time of involvement with each other and a response to the Word which had been proclaimed. We called our gathering, "The Celebration of the Christian Life." Most of the adult members were involved in an adult study group.

My personal life was not exactly running on all eight cylinders. Paul's writing about Christians being new creatures in Jesus, the Christ through the resurrection, grasped my mind but did little for me as a person. I did not feel I was a new person. The experience with the Rev. Mr. Judas had not helped me with my own sexual struggles. The turmoil within continued as I wrestled with my gayness, while trying to keep it a secret. There were storm clouds on the horizon. I did not have the foggiest notion what the future would hold.

THE SHADOW OF THE CROSS

Once again my continuing education came to the rescue. I took a course given by Professor Neil Hamilton which challenged my understanding of the history of the early Christian church. I had always thought the Christian church had existed as a unit tied together with a common understanding of who Jesus of Nazareth was. Up to this point my continuing education had exposed me to the writing of the Hellenistic Jewish Church found in the synoptic Gospels (Matthew, Mark, Luke), and the writings of Paul. In this course of Professor Hamilton, I was introduced to the Palestinian Jewish church. It was composed of people who were Jewish in culture and in religion, but had departed from the Jewish religion and were following the teachings of Jesus of Nazareth. The message of Jesus was put in the social and historical setting in which he lived.

"Jesus was a Jew and was convinced Yahweh had created everything, and it was good. This goodness which was stated at the end of the first chapter of Genesis had never been overturned. Common life was good and you did not have to change it into something immaterial or spiritual as did Paul and the Hellenistic Jewish Church. Jesus saw the untransformed historical life as the place which was filled with the grace of Yahweh.

"Jesus was an itinerant preacher, and that was that. People came to Jesus out of individual decisions to turn from the way they had been living to follow his teachings in their personal lives. When we look closely at his work, there is no organization. He did not have twelve disciples. He seemed to be prescribing life for individuals. He related to individuals. He had a conversation here and there. The rich young ruler came with a question and got an answer. Jesus healed a person here and there. At first glance it appears the ethical teachings of Jesus were answers to questions in an individual's life and not the structuring of a community. It is no wonder people who consider themselves primarily Bible-believing Christians, good Protestants, came out with a piety which is devoid of any social concern.

"But if we think Jesus was not concerned with social change we have missed the whole impact of his teaching. This is what orthodox Christianity has done. All of the privatism and individualism made sense only because it was given under a massive suggestion and concern for the arrangement, namely the Kingdom of Yahweh. This was the presupposition, the reason for everything else. Jesus came preaching that Yahweh was about to establish a whole new culture, a new life, and if a person wanted to be part of this new movement he had better get on his bandwagon. The

Kingdom of Yahweh was a blatantly political concept and this was the reason the people of Jesus' day got excited about his preaching. They needed to turn from their way of life and go against the grain of their present culture. They could afford to do this because they figured the present set-up would not last long.

"The purpose of Yahweh was accomplished but not in the way Jesus said it would happen. There was a shift from Yahweh as the agent of change to human beings as the agents of change. The only difference is that we are limited in our powers. But limited as we are, history belongs to us in the sense that if anything at all can be accomplished, we must be the agents of change. The greatest heresy of the traditional approach to the Christian faith has been to lose sight of the political aspect of Jesus' message and its full sociological scope. The church has been so preoccupied with programs to increase personal virtue and piety that it has trivialized the range of concerns Jesus attributed to Yahweh. In effect, modern Christianity has replaced the Kingdom of Yahweh with private religious experiences and being shipped off to heaven after death.

"In Jesus' vision of the Kingdom of Yahweh we have a clear enough idea to provide guidance and direction in the particular issues in our lives. We see Jesus associating with the religious and economic outcasts of his time because in the new system they would have full status. The kingdom would eliminate illness, so Jesus healed. The kingdom would give people power over their lives, so Jesus attacked those who were demon-possessed and gave them life. The kingdom would likely judge men of exalted economic and religious status, so Jesus scorned the wealthy and pious. When asked what was the important commandment, Jesus responded with a vision of a kingdom highlighted with the 'agape' of Yahweh, and 'agape' for one's neighbor. The kingdom would come in, but it would come in through men and women who would be the agents through whom change would take place.

"Given that, what do we do with our inhumanity against each other? Is the traditional answer that we are inherently evil, in need of being saved, in need of a new nature, the answer? No! Jesus did not call for or offer a new human nature as the condition for entering the kingdom. That is Pauline and Hellenistic theology. Jesus called for repentance. Repentance is more than feeling sorry for what we have done and then turning around and doing it all over again. Repentance is an act of our will. It is turning around and going in a new direction.

"This implies the problem is not located in our nature, but in the direction of our lives. Remaking our human nature is simply not available, but help to change the direction of our lives is an open option to all of us. It means understanding that we have taken the things of this world and put them together in the wrong way, and we can change that.

"When Jesus came into the temple and overturned the tables of the money changers, he was literally closing the Jewish National Bank. He closed the whole business operation. No wonder people were upset. Jesus, a good Jew, saw the temple as one of the main places where the people brought their religion to expression. It was important for the Jews of Jesus' day to get ready for the coming change in the arrangements Yahweh would institute on the Day of the Lord.

"Did the people understand what Jesus was doing? Probably. Most of them believed the Kingdom of Yahweh was coming, and it would be a change in the arrangements. Most of them did not believe Jesus was the one to do this, and they did not believe the change would be for the benefit of the poor. Most of the Jews saw Jesus as one who was getting out of line. He was getting to be impossible. Whenever a person comes along who wants to change the economic situation he is considered a danger. Any culture or arrangement can stand religious heretics. They are easily dealt with. But when you have a religious and economic heretic in the same person, that is too much, and it is important to get rid of that person.

"From the point of view of the early Christian Church, Yahweh did bring in the Day of the Lord, but the promise was fulfilled in a new and different way. Human beings, not some angel or super person, would be the instruments through which any changes in the arrangement would take place. Before we take off on any change we must ask ourselves if we are willing to take the consequences of our action."

This understanding of Jesus made him more human and less divine. It supported my contention that the early Christian church had difficulty with the Divinity of Jesus, and the church of our time has forgotten his humanness. Professor Hamilton's lectures helped me put these two aspects of Jesus into focus. What really made sense to me was that a person did not have to become a new creature to be Christian. All we had to do was to change the direction of our lives. This helped me as I struggled with being a homosexual. Changing the direction of my life was a real possibility.

Another idea from Hamilton on which I focused was the suggestion that the sayings of Jesus had been remembered and repeated. When it came time to write about Jesus, the writers took the sayings and provided the context. This was really the only approach they had, because they were writing a generation or so later following Jesus' life. They were preserving the teachings of Jesus, not so they would have something to look back upon with reverence, but because the sayings solved the problems of their own and their communities' lives. But different communities used the teachings in different ways. In the story of the rich young ruler, we see how the Palestinian Jewish and Hellenistic Jewish churches used this material.

"We begin with the Jewish Palestinian church. Here comes the rich young ruler. That is the Jewish church located culturally in Jewish thought, and not much in Roman or Greek. The rich young ruler is a model of Jewish piety. The problem of the Palestinian church is their Jewish brothers do not see what is so special about Jewish Christians, so the writer is going to tell them. This young man wants eternal life. He has done everything his religion required of him from his youth on, so the young man deserves eternal life. 'No, not quite,' says the Palestinian church. There is something more. 'If you want to enter the Kingdom of Yahweh there is another requirement. You must become poor in order to enter the Kingdom of Yahweh. You need to be on the side of the new arrangement which Yahweh is about to introduce.'

"The Kingdom of Yahweh would be a massive turnover in the arrangement of the society and especially the economical realm. It would be a society in which the blessings would be for the poor, not the wealthy. If you wanted to be in this new Kingdom, you had better share it with the people for whom it is designed. The writer was not suggesting being poor was good for your spirituality, as we thought in later years. The Palestinian Christians were willing to become poor because in the coming Kingdom of Yahweh, the poor would be the ones who would make it. The overall arching model of piety in the coming reign was to be poor. Since this great change was not far off in the future, they could afford to stand against the present arrangement.

"The Hellenistic Jewish church did not accept this idea of poverty. They took this saying and made a few changes. The Hellenistic Jewish church explored a riskier way. So Jesus says, 'With men it is impossible, but not with Yahweh, for all things are possible for Yahweh. It is even possible for a camel to go through the eye of a needle.' (1) The Hellenistic Jewish church recognized the impossible possibility.

"How are they going to get out of this impossible saying of Jesus? How are they going to stay with their affluence at least to some extent and still keep this saying of Jesus about those who will be caught with their wealth in the end? Peter, their spokesman, says, 'Lord, we have left everything and followed.' Jesus replied, "I tell you this: there is no one who has left house, or brothers, or sisters, or mother, or father, for my sake or for the gospel who will not now receive a hundredfold in this time. . '" (2) In other words if you have to drop your affluence for the sake of the mission, but in the fulfillment of the mission you are brought back into affluence, that is okay."

"Mark does not let it end here. He throws in a clinker. He reminds the Hellenistic Jewish church that they cannot forget the implication of the crucifixion as a model for Christian life and piety, and neither can we. The death of Jesus is a model for all Christians in all ages."

In the adult study groups I went into more detail comparing the way the writers of the Palestinian Jewish, Hellenistic Jewish, and Gentile churches provided the context for the teachings of Jesus. As we began to understand this methodology of the New Testament writers I began toying with the idea that we in the First Presbyterian church of Coos Bay should take those sayings of Jesus which had meaning for us and put them into a new context. At that time in our journey, however, no one was ready to do that. It takes time for old ideas to die before new ones can take their place.

Despite all of the new theological ideas which had been expressed in the sermons and explored in the discussion groups since "That

Sunday," I began to understand we, as a congregation, were still too steeped in salvation theology. It stood in the way of our understanding that before we could enjoy the glories of Easter we must first experience the crucifixion. This experience was beginning to make itself known in the life of the Coos Bay church. This was more than some theological idea. The ordeal of dying began in the life of the congregation and in myself, as their pastor and as a person.

From "That Sunday" to the end of 1969 our focus had been an attempt to find a new name for "God." This did not happen. The footprints in the sand had taken us to the life of Jesus, focusing on the resurrection. Now the idea of the crucifixion began to assert itself. We began to understand that, before we could enjoy the glories of Easter, we had to experience Good Friday. That was crucial. These two events were two sides of the same coin. Even before it was expressed in words, a personalized Good Friday was quietly being experienced in the life of the congregation, in myself as their pastor, and in my marriage.

In addition to the theology of the God-up-there, a second foundation of traditional Western Christian doctrine needed to be attacked, subdued, and put on the shelf. That was the Salvation Theology which promoted the idea that Jesus died for me, and no matter how badly I might mess up my life, on my death bed I can call on Jesus to save me. No Way. Here are the arguments against salvation theology which I presented to the church.

"Augustine was the architect of Western Christianity. He taught that all of humanity had fallen into the depths of sin and were doomed to hell. This fall was not simply a deficiency in our nature as humans beings; we had become less than human. Augustine was the person who negated the goodness of the creation story, something the Old Testament writers had not done. In Augustine's thinking there was no

120

hope for any of us. Well, not quite. The God-up-there keeps an account of our good deeds and our bad deeds, and when life on this earth ends he tallies our totals to see if the good outweighs the bad. We can reduce the bad weight by confessing our sins and depending on the death of Jesus to wipe them out. Our access to this plan is possible only because the death of Jesus gives us a 'new nature.' The gracious God-up-there still loved us enough to have sent Jesus to save us from our sins.

"This idea is reinforced every Christmas. We hear and sing carols throughout the Christmas season reminding us that Jesus was born to save us from our sins. Interestingly, another element in Christmas which on the surface seems to be at odds with this sin and salvation message, actually reflects the same message. That element is Santa Claus. Christmas has always been a strange mixture of Jesus and Santa. In reality Santa is also good salvation theology. Santa, the man with the long white bread, is up at the North Pole making a list, checking it twice, trying to find out who's naughty or nice. From this perspective Jesus and Santa are in the same ball game. Santa is a tool grown-ups use at Christmas time to help keep the kids in line.

"One snowy day shortly before Christmas a school bus driver was having trouble with his passengers, who ranged from the first through the fourth grade. After trying all the tricks of the trade to get the kids to calm down, he finally pulled off the road and stopped. Grabbing the two-way radio, he yelled, 'This is bus no. 4 and I've had it. I want to talk to Santa Claus. Repeat, get me Santa Claus at the North Pole. Over.'

"Back at the office the dispatcher turned with a blank expression on his face to some of the other drivers and said, 'That guy's lost his mind. He's flipped.'

But another driver, sensing what was happening, grabbed

the mike. A deep-bellied voice filled the buss. 'Ho! Ho! Ho,! bus no. 4. This is Santa Clause at the north Pole. What seems to be your trouble?'

'Santa,' replied the driver, 'I'm having a lot of trouble with a bunch of usually nice kids. What shall I do?'

Santa's voice boomed throughout the bus, 'You tell those kids to sit down and behave, or there'll be no Santa for them. And I don't want them to make you bother me again. I'm busy getting presents ready.'

Later that day the driver of bus no.4 said, 'You coulda heard a pin drop for the rest of the route.'

"Santa may be the tool used by adults to control kids, but 'Jesus died for me,' is the control used by the institutional church to control its members; it is through the church that we retain access to this system of confession and forgiveness. We are reminded of this in the carols we sing at Christmas. Jesus was born to die for us so that at the time of our death, if we have confessed our sins, our souls can be shipped off to heaven.

"Salvation theology is not the emphasis in the New Testament. The essence of the Christmas event was that the Word of Yahweh had become flesh, in this Jesus of Nazareth, who dwelt among us. We could say, 'Yahweh's love was let loose in this world.' The essence of the incarnation was 'agape.' Yahweh's 'love' was let loose at Christmas time, and this 'love' has not been withdrawn.

"Jesus did not teach that our human nature needed to be changed. It was the direction of our lives which needed to be changed. The evil which is present and abounds in our lives is there because we have put them there. These negative aspects of human life can be controlled. We can change the direction of our lives from the negative to the positive. To be Christian is to take seriously our humanity and our part in the realm of history, economics, politics and culture. We are responsible for both the good and the evil we do.

"The impact of the Incarnation is that the God-up-there came down and became the God-in-our-midst. That is the wonderful message of Christmas. And it is the Easter event that gives meaning to Christmas. That cute little baby grew up into a man, a man who showed us what the 'love' of Yahweh meant in human terms. He stood against the conventions of his time, and they killed him. But that 'love' could not be contained in the grave. That 'love' came alive and was experienced in the lives of the disciples. The Gospels are the record of the meaning of that 'love' in the lives of the authors and the congregations to whom they wrote. Yahweh's love was let loose at that first Christmas and has not been withdrawn or wiped out. It is still being expressed in human lives today."

Talking about Christmas reminds me of snow. Before we moved to Coos Bay someone from the church had sent us a bundle of materials from the Chamber of Commerce proclaiming the wonders and joys of living on the coast of Southern Oregon. One claim which made an impression on my memory was that it never snowed in Coos Bay. What a joy to hear that. We had just experienced a winter in Wisconsin where we had over forty days of below zero temperatures. January gave us twenty-one days in a row of below zero weather and a couple of days which began at thirty-eight below. School was not canceled because of the cold, so we bundled up the kids until all you could see were coats, scarfs, mittens, and boots. They looked lost under those clothes as they waddled down the sidewalk. Even though two sides of the garage shared walls with the house, some water in the garage under the car froze. When driving the car, I was sure I had square tires. We were glad to move to any climate where it did not get so cold.

We had also had a lot of snow that year. So much snow had fallen and been pushed up by the snow plows that it was almost impossible for a person approaching an intersection to see any cars coming from the right or left. Many of us had tied ribbons on the antennas of our cars for safety. I have not forgotten that winter.

On top of all of this snow, mother nature dumped another thirty inches of snow one night. The next morning I tried to get out to shovel the snow. I tried the front door. It was snowed shut. I tried the back door, and after much pushing and shoving I succeeded in opening it just enough to be able to squeeze through the opening and onto the porch, thanks to my narrow waistline. I begin to shovel us free. My driveway was not very wide, only about half again the width of an average car's width, and about two and a half cars in length. It was not a big driveway, but it took me all day to clear it to the street and the front sidewalks. I had no sooner finished when the snow plow came through and filled up the driveway with packed snow, which is almost impossible to shovel out. I quietly swore.

It was wonderful news to read that Coos Bay did not have snow. We moved to Coos Bay and what happened? We had snow for the next ten years. So much for the Chamber of Commerce's false claim. After the second year of dealing with snow in a town built on hills, I purchased some snow tires.

I performed a wedding one Saturday night after Christmas. The reception was held at the bride's home. I looked out a window and saw snowflakes falling. They were not melting when they hit the ground. I checked a little later, and there was no sign the snow was going to stop. I took off for home. The next morning I got up and looked out of the front window. Behold, my eyes were greeted with a winter wonderland even Disney could not have surpassed.

Fourteen inches of snow had fallen on the city of Coos Bay and surrounding territory. I decided to walk down to the church and have it open just in case someone tried to get there. No one did. The City of Coos Bay had also listened to the Chamber of Commerce and was not prepared to handle the snow. We simply waited for warmer weather to melt it away. Two weeks later I went out to the ranch and found thirty inches of snow still on the ground. To my surprise the house was still standing, but the barn had collapsed from the weight of the snow. I had a good supply of building materials for any future construction.

The weather returned to normal in time for me to attend a meeting of the Synod's Worship Committee. Again I brought up the issue of the doctrine of God. This time when the chairman insisted that all I was raising was a matter of semantics, the campus pastor at the University of Oregon, came to my aid. He said, "It is more than semantics. It involves theology. It involves the doctrine of God, an issue which college students are raising and is something the Presbyterian Church needs to address." The committee planned some workshops focusing on the theology of God.

The workshops began with a worship service which I led. I followed the new order of worship in The Book of Common Worship, Provisional Services recently published by the Presbyterian Church (U.S.A.). I began the sermon, "All that we have done thus far has been very religious, but not necessarily Christian." That got their attention. I continued by attacking the traditional doctrine of God, followed by some ideas concerning who Jesus was and might be. The sermon was a quick review of the theological journey of the Coos Bay church. I did not bring it to any conclusion. I just stopped and the people were sent off to discussion groups. And discuss they did.

I went from group to group and listened for a few moments. In one group was the pastor of a large Presbyterian Church in Oregon who was a former moderator of the General Assembly and an authority figure in theology. He shook his head and indicated that I was out in left field and did not have a leg to stand on. What he did not know was that some of my thinking had been influenced by a sermon he had given. While I did not impress him, the minds of others had stretched. This was evident when the groups returned and shared their responses to what I had given.

Returning to Coos Bay I decided to study the parables of Jesus. The parables were a key method Jesus used in his teaching. His message proclaimed that the long-awaited day of salvation was about to arrive. The coming reign of Yahweh was just around the corner. Jesus pointed the minds of his disciples not toward the horrors of the end of the present age, but to the signs of the coming of a new age, To help people discern the signs, Jesus used parables. Some of the people accepted what Jesus had to say. Others dismissed him as some silly, impudent teacher. The idea of interpreting the Parables and sayings of Jesus in light of the coming Day of the Lord was a new approach to me.

"The parable known as the Prodigal Son has taken its place in Western culture. The forgiveness of the father of his prodigal son is well known. This is salvation theology at its best. The motive is there, but it is not the teaching of the parable. The punch line concerns the elder brother who has returned from an exhausting day in the fields. Hearing all the noise he asks one of the servants, 'What's going on?' The servant tells him and the elder brother blows his top. He refuses to have anything to do with the celebration and stays outside and sulks. He had every right to be angry and out-of-sorts. The father joins the elder son and reminds him that he, too, has access to what the father had. The statement made no impression on the elder son and he continues to sulk. (3)
"The context which prompted this parable was that

tax-gatherers and other bad characters were crowding in to listen to Jesus and in the process were probably pushing the scribes and Pharisees aside. The implication of the parable is that the elder son represents the scribes and Pharisees who were out-of-sorts that Jesus would even speak to such trash. They were offended to hear Jesus imply that when the Kingdom of Yahweh arrived it would be for the undeserving, the outcast, the poor. As far as the Pharisees were concerned those bad characters were 'sinners.' In the New Testament the word for 'sinner' is used in a very technical way. The word meant (a) a person who led an immoral life, (b) a person who followed a dishonorable occupation which usually involved immoral dishonesty. Those people were deprived of their civil rights. They were 'sinners,' according to the Pharisees, because they were not religious people.

"The Pharisees were the good, stable, religious people who tried to keep the religious life of Israel on the right track. They did not try to make the Jewish religion difficult. It was the opposite. They came up with many difficult requirements to fulfill the law and in the process they made it almost impossible for the law to be fulfilled They put themselves in the position of being a judge. Those who followed their rules and regulations were the 'righteous people' and those who did not were 'sinners' − in our language, the bad guys.

"The seduction of such a position was that their goodness and righteousness led them to scorn others. They were offended with the idea that the love and mercy of Yahweh went out to people who refused to fit their religious mold. In this parable Jesus compares the Pharisees with the older brother and reminds them Yahweh's love was for all.

"The parable was a defense of Jesus' teaching about who would be in the Kingdom of Yahweh. It would include those who had kept the rules. It would also include those who had defied the rules, had come to their senses and realized they had gone off in the wrong direction in their lives, and made the necessary change. Jesus did not call for a new human life but for a radical turning from the pursuit of the ordinary ends of life to the pursuit of the ends of the Kingdom of Yahweh. A life not restrictive, but open; not of safety, but filled with risk; not closed, always open.

Easter Sunday 1970 was the beginning of the end. It is difficult for me to believe I really gave that sermon. I had broken one of my cardinal rules of preaching. A preacher does not take advantage of a captured audience to tell them off. As I reread that sermon, I remembered the intense debate which had taken place within me as I prepared it. My internal struggle started quietly on Monday and slowly increased as the week progressed. One argument went, "If you say what you have written, it will go over like a lead balloon. If you say what you have prepared, those once-a-year people will take offense. If you want a congregation left, you had better tone it down." But another thought kept saying, "Do not worry about those once-a-year people. They are not the core of this church. They really do not know what has taken place and do not contribute to its life. They do not count." And the debate continued every day until I stood up to give the sermon. At that moment it ended. I knew I had to give what I had prepared no matter what the consequences. I was angry when I gave that sermon. And I am feeling some of that anger even now as I write this, many years later.

I gave a quick review of the theological material we had covered in the previous four years and especially the meaning of the Easter Event. Many who were present at that service had made the comment that they no longer knew what I was talking about. They had not said this to me, but to others who told me. The third paragraph in that sermon went:

"If this does not make sense to you, it is because we as a

congregation are in the process of unlearning most of what we have been taught all our lives about the Resurrection. It is easy to tear down religious ideas, and many of you may have heard that part well enough, but you have not been around to hear the concepts and ideas which were put in place of the old.

"Anyone attending a church service once or twice a year could not possibly know what has been happening in the life of this congregation for the past four-and-a-half years. If you were a right-handed person and lost your right hand in an accident, what would you do? You would either get an artificial limb, or you would have to learn how to use your left hand. In either case, you would learn how to use it through day-to-day therapy. The new skill would not come by working at it only at Easter, Mother's Day , or Christmas Sunday."

I could have stopped right there, sung the closing hymn and given the benediction. I do not think any of the once-a-year attendees heard one word I had said. I suppose if I were in their shoes I would not have heard anything either. To add insult to injury, I had made a great change in the physical setup of the church. The traditional format had the pews facing the front of the church where people looked at the choir, the communion table, the preacher and the backs of the heads of people sitting in front of them.

Robert R. and a few other men from the congregation had helped me move the communion table to the center of the church and put the pews on both sides facing each other. We slanted them toward the middle. This was not done in silence. There was a good deal of joking going back and forth between them while they grunted and groaned moving those heavy pews. Most of the comments were aimed at me. If this had not happened, I would have been worried. They were used to teasing each other and me whenever we were together. When it was finished they thought it looked nice. It sure was different.

To me, this was as close to a church-in-the-round as I could get in a rectangular building. This arrangement supported the idea of the congregation being "The Christ" and gathered around the Lord's table when they came to worship. In this arrangement the congregation was seated on each side of the communion table facing each other. They had spent all of their lives looking at the backs of heads.. Now they had to look at the faces of people who were looking at them. .That was too much for the once-a-year people. Without the background of the theology of the journey they really were lost with this arrangement.

That change almost did us in. Even the faithful, those who returned after that Easter service, who kept the church going, did not like that arrangement. As people arrived, they sat in the side facing the front as they had always done. Since our attendance was small they could all fit in the back half. With the exception of the choir, none were brave enough to sit on the front side of the building facing the people sitting opposite them. My marvelous idea was a total flop. After a very short time, we returned the communion table to the front of the church. The pews went back into two sections with a center aisle, but they were slanted towards the center aisle. I did make some other changes. I stopped wearing my robe (it has been in moth balls ever since). When it came time for the sermon, I left the pulpit and stood on the same level as the people.

After that Easter Sunday the once-a-year people did not return. Attendance dropped to the seventies and eighties. What the Coos Bay Presbyterian congregation had been when I had arrived was no more. It had died. What I did not know then was that no other response was possible. Good Friday – death – was not some event in the life of Jesus safely tucked away in history and recalled when we read about it from the scriptures. Instead, the belief that whatever happened to Jesus in the New Testament would happen to us was becoming a reality. We did not know what was happening; we were simply aware we were not the same group of people who had begun the journey. Only a few remained from the original congregation plus those who had been drawn to what we had become formed the core of the new congregation.

The last paragraph of the Easter sermon hit the nail on the head to those whose ears were open:

"In the process of taking risks we might be wrong as to what must be done, but it is better to be wrong and understand this later than to have sat on our hands and done nothing, or to have sat in the pews Sunday after Sunday and then gone home and said, 'So what?' The individual Christian is not a possibility. A person becomes a Christian only in the presence of, confrontation with, and living together with other Christians. We are the church today only as we are willing to endure the painful process of 'unlearning' past theological concepts and replacing them with new thoughts and ideas. We have never been the 'saved ones.' We have been called to be 'the saving ones.' "

Fortunately I no longer stood at the doorway to the church. I stood at the back of the sanctuary near the entrance which made me available if anyone wanted to make any comments. This arrangement saved the people from having to face me after the service. It gave them an out if they did not like what they had heard. I did not get any compliments on that Easter Sunday's sermon.

A few years before this fateful Easter Sunday my son was in junior high and a member of the band. They were selling magazine subscriptions to raise money. As dutiful father I ordered "Organic

Gardening and Farming." I thought it would be just another magazine on gardening, but I was in for a surprise. It was a new approach based on the idea of feeding the soil and not the plant. The magazine promoted the idea of gardening as close to the "way of nature," and opposed to the chemical method used in modern agriculture.

The magazine contended that in its natural state, earth is a finely defined system of checks and balances. Life is found in many a varied form, each specialized and together make a whole. Where this balance is kept, life continues and flourishes. When this balance is disrupted, as modern farming does, the unexpected is more difficult to handle and the massive use of chemicals is not the answer. This was given about two weeks after that disastrous Easter Sunday. Looking back on the timing of the that sermon, maybe I thought I could save my congregation at the same time I was saving the world. It did not stop the dying in the congregation or in my professional life.

Two weeks after the sermon on ecology, I gave a state-of-the-congregation message, even if it was in May, not January. This time there was no inner battle over what to say. There was no anger, some frustration, but no anger; I was sharing with the "remnant" of the congregation the past, the present and what the future might be.

This should not have been given in a sermon. It would have been much better in the adult study groups. Once again I abused the privilege of the pulpit. I felt I needed to get a few things off my chest. I started with a good summation of the theological journey and then turned to my frustrations. I began:

"The ministry is not like other professions. The lawyer knows if the case was won or lost. The doctor knows if the treatment was successful. The dentist can show you the tooth which was removed. The architect points with pride to the building he or she designed. But as a minister, I have no real knowledge of whether or not what I have preached or taught, since we started this journey, has become a reality in the life of anyone in this congregation . All the words of wisdom I have sprinkled upon your heads have been for naught if they have not brought forth a style of living which enables you to bring forth fruit. I can talk about 'agape' all I want on Sunday morning, but unless this 'agape' is translated into concern for our neighbor, our community, our families, our nation – you name it – they remain just that – nice sounding words. I have gotten hints that some of you have taken these words and ideas seriously and have gone into our community to function as 'Christ,' and that is good.

That much was okay, but not the rest of the sermon. Those who were there listened with patience and put up with my frustration. I do not have any idea what they thought. No one said anything following the service. No one suggested it was time for me to leave and find another church. I think this was because the members were as befuddled as I was. The drop in attendance on Sunday morning had really gotten to me. The members still attending were also disturbed by the loss of members but did not know what to do. I felt I had found the essence of the message of the New Testament writers. To me the message was a matter of life and death, but not many were present to hear it. The drop in attendance and loss of members to other churches indicated that there had been a cost to us. As their pastor this was difficult for me to handle. I knew something was happening to me over which I did not have much control. I could only respond, and at that time my response was not very good. In New Testament theological terms I was dying, not physically, but as their pastor and their leader. I was rebelling against having to die.

I know now it was my ego which had gotten in the way. I wanted to avoid all the problems which had confronted Moses as he lead those stiff-necked people to the promised land. I did not want to remember that Moses had been denied entrance to the promised land. I did not want to go through Gethsemane, or the cross as Jesus had done. I was frustrated, angry, and dumbfounded that people were leaving. Although we had not gotten anywhere with the doctrine of 'God,' we had found our way in understanding who this Jesus had been to the early Christian churches, and what Jesus could mean to us. I began to understand people did not want to hear about taking risks and taking responsibility for their lives. Remember that workshop on *One Flew Over the Cuckoo's Nest* where I had been accused by another minister of being conceited? He was right. I was conceited, but in a different way than he thought.

After all, if I had been willing to change, I felt the members of the congregation should also be willing to change and follow me like blind sheep. That was not what many of them wanted. Attendance continued to drop and hit an all-time low one summer evening. Would you believe only twenty-five? That made an impression. It hurt deeply. At the same time the inadequacy of Salvation Theology remained apparent. Jesus did not come to my rescue. Instead we understood the theological meaning of getting out of the boat. We had to face the consequences of this great change. If people did not want to take a risk or pay the price, then that was something I had to accept even if I did not want to. In plain words, there is no way to the joy and glory of Easter except through the experience of Good Friday. Death was on its way in the life of the congregation, in my life as a minister, and in my marriage.

GOOD FRIDAY

DEATH AND DYING

Some memories are not hidden deep within, needing a great amount of energy to be recalled. They lie just beneath the surface, waiting for a chance to rise and stare us in the face. One such memory is September, 1970. For me the church year started after Labor Day. School began, members of the congregation returned from their summer vacations, and all of the civic organizations were in full swing. No matter how badly the church program might have ended in May, we could always start anew in September. But not September of 1970. Throughout the summer I had brooded over what had happened. My creative mind seemed to be at its wits end. As September loomed on the horizon, I did not see how we as a congregation would ever get through the coming year. Most of the traditional programs of the past had ceased or were in a period of transition. No one was sure of what was going to happen.

For the first time in my ministry I did not look forward to September. I did not have any energy. I was depressed. I was not functioning as I had.

Throughout my ministry I had kept good records. On Monday morning I would record the date of the Sunday just passed, the title of the sermon, the hymns, the scripture passage, the responsive reading, the attendance, and any unusual event which might have taken place. I no longer cared about keeping that information. Fortunately, I had kept the bulletins, so I did have that information, with the exception of the attendance. I knew that it had fallen.

Lurking in the back of my mind was the taunting accusation that a minister's success was measured by how many people attended services on a Sunday morning, and how well the programs were

135

supported. From this perspective, I had failed. I had expected a drop in attendance when we began our journey, but not the landslide which had taken place. I did not want to accept the fact that preaching which challenges a person to think might not be what many people wanted to hear. It was a very dark time in my life.

"Dead" is not the word. I was dying. Dying is a verb, an experience which occurs over a period of time. It happened to me, my marriage, my ministry, and the congregation. Since "That Sunday," I had discovered that the important words in the Bible are verbs, not nouns. A noun is a word which defines an object, and we can agree on the definition. A verb is an experience and cannot be defined. The congregation and I were in the midst of dying to the past. It was an experience which we could not define, but we could talk about it, and even if we did not use the same words, we knew what the other person meant.

There were two groups in the congregation: those in the adult study groups who were interested in the new forms of worship and the change in theology; and those who were more or less holding onto the past. As a congregation we were not sure who we were, how we should function, or where we were going. Reading about Jesus in the New Testament was one thing. Having to live those experiences was quite another. We had emphasized Easter. Beginning in September 1970, we began to understand that Good Friday came before Easter, and we could not avoid it. I have not forgotten September of 1970. What fascinates me as I write this is that our dying and coming alive went hand in hand.

One indication of dying and coming alive at the same time was in the life of the congregation. Those who were still active found the journey was important in their lives. They took seriously the idea that if "Yahweh" was out in the world working, then as Christians, they must be involved in the world. In study groups and in our

Celebration of The Christian Life, we supported each other in our differences and our oneness. We were aware that our Celebration of the Christian Life was not left in the sanctuary, but was to lead us to reach out into the life of the community.

The Day Care program which had been on a part-time basis at the Pacific View Presbyterian Church near us was moved to our church and became full time. This was a joint venture with other churches. Each church was responsible to staff the day care one day of the week. The first full-time director hired did not last beyond the first year. In the second year Ed was hired, and in a short time he had the program on its feet. He had a wonderful ability to work with volunteers. He was gay. We became friends. This friendship has lasted through the years. He has helped in the writing of this book.

It was the adult study groups which kept us going. The people continued to wrestle with the theological concepts we had encountered in our journey. I began to realize the once-a-year people did not matter, and those who had transferred their membership were better off where they had gone. There was a core of dedicated people receiving what they wanted. Sunday morning was important, and a new pattern began to emerge. Choir practice continued on Sunday morning. Since I was directing the choir and was the first person to arrive, I would start the coffee so it would be ready when the people came. Members of the church began to arrive early to listen to the choir, have a cup of coffee, chitchat, and welcome any visitors. Sunday morning began with the coffee hour, moved to celebrate our Christian life, and ended with a second coffee hour. We installed a coffee cup rack on a wall and each member had a place for his or her cup.

So great was my feeling of having failed I did not remember having anything important to give in my sermons. I was wrong. Going through them I discovered the sermons were about some of the difficult demands of the Christian Faith. For instance, one is found in Paul's letter to the Romans and reads:

"And, as we know, all things work together for good for those who love God and are called according to his purpose.' (Romans 8:28, 29). A seminary professor had been talking about this passage and stopped to take a breath. A student said, 'Do you really believe all things work together for good? All the pain, suffering, and misery, do you?' The professor replied, 'I do. What happens to a person might not seem to be good in and of itself, but a person could make them work together for good.' That afternoon the professor and his wife were involved in an automobile accident. She was killed and he was left a cripple. He sent for the president of the college and said, 'Tell my students Romans 8:28 still holds good.' He died a year later. On his tombstone they inscribed the words from Romans 8:28.

"The second half of that verse has been used as a argument for predestination. For many people it says that whatever happens to them in life is meant to be and there is nothing they can do about it. It was all determined by the God-up-there. This is not much different from the Stoic idea of fate. When tragedy strikes the burning question is 'How do we handle it? 'The Stoics said, 'Accept it, or rebel. But if you rebelled you would only get hurt.' Paul's answer to this question was that in the risen Christ a new age had begun and Christians were the avant garde. They would bring in this new creation. It would not be a picnic. It would come through great difficulties. Paul ended this discussion with the assurance that nothing in this world could separate Christians from the 'love' of Yahweh.

"In Paul's thinking it is not what happens to us that counts, but how we respond. 'Why did this happen to me?' is not a proper question. Any tragedy can become a stepping stone, an opportunity for growth, especially in the spiritual realm. No matter how shattering, how terrifying, how horrible the disaster might be, adversity offers us the opportunity of affirming life, not death. The same promise given by Paul to the early Christians is still valid today. There is nothing in this world which can separate us from the love of Yahweh in Christ Jesus our Lord. Yahweh is not interested in death, but in life.

As I went through the sermons I gave that fall I began to understand why I did not remember having anything important to say. From hindsight I can see that, as my world seemed to be falling apart, the sermons I was giving were answers to my own situation. What was happening was not the important thing, but rather how I handled the situation. The loss in membership and the collapse of the program could be an opportunity for growth.

Another idea from the writing of Paul helped us to handle our death and dying.

"'I appeal to you therefore, brethren, by the mercies of God, to present your bodies as a living sacrifice, holy and acceptable to God, which is your spiritual worship. Do not be conformed to this world but be transformed by the renewal of your mind, that you may prove what is the will of God, what is good and acceptable and perfect.' (1) Christians are called to be a living sacrifice. It is obvious a living sacrifice is different from being killed and offered as a burnt offering. We are whole, complete persons with the power of renewing the direction of our lives which means doing what is beneficial, upright, and well pleasing toward others. For Paul, worship was a perpetual, never-ending activity. The Christian's life is a constant act of worship. Worship is not confined to a sanctuary."

These are difficult words. These are not words of comfort in the usual sense. This is not advice for someone who has been deeply hurt and is expecting sympathy. These words helped the members and myself get through the difficult time we faced. These words of Paul gave comfort. We knew no one would come to our rescue. Whatever the future held, it would depend on how well we handled our dying and death.

Help did come. In November the Synod's Committee on Worship sent me to a workshop on new forms of worship being held at the seminary in San Anselmo. I was sent because I was doing more in new forms of worship than anyone else. In this conference I would experience that all things do work together for good for those who love the Lord.

The first session was very standard. We introduced ourselves and gave something about our backgrounds and why we had come. The leaders presented the format for the week which included attending a production of the stage play "Hair." That sounded fine, and I was looking forward to it. Just before we left for San Francisco to attend the play, a handsome young minister joined the group. His good looks caught my attention. He had arrived late and was not at the first session, and therefore had not been introduced. The group left for the play almost immediately after his arrival, but I knew instinctively our lives would come together.

At the theater I was seated in the front row, on the left side of the center aisle. I could not have been closer to the action unless I had been sitting on the stage. I was not interested in rock-and-roll music and wondered how I would last through the whole production. As it progressed I became more interested and more involved. I was caught up in the music and the message of the play itself, but it was the half-naked beautiful male bodies which had all of my attention. When it was over the audience was invited up on the stage, and there I was on the stage talking with the actors. It was something I would not have done in my wildest dreams.

The next morning's session began with a discussion of "Hair." It soon turned into a discussion of sex. I do not remember what I said, but probably something to the effect that I was not too concerned about who went to bed with whom, but I was very concerned about why anyone went to bed with anyone else. It was motive that counted, not the act in and of itself.

After a while the leader said that we would engage in exercises where we would be touching each other. Most conferences, at that time, had a session where the participants were taught it was okay for people, and men in particular, to touch, hug, and be more physical with each other. But I often wondered if the leaders knew that such close physical contact might also be very sexual to some people. Because of this, I had avoided any conference where I thought such an encounter might take place. A conference on new forms of worship seemed quite safe. Suddenly I was confronted with having to be physical with other men.

The first couple of exercises did not present a problem. I began to breathe a little easier. Then the leader told us we were going to get more personal. We would pair off, hold hands, and look into each other's eyes. That was precisely what I did not want to do! Fortunately, none of the ministers in the group were attractive, except the young man who had arrived late.

I did not want to risk looking into his eyes or holding his hands. I took a quick look around for the ugliest man in the group. Before I could move, the young minister was sitting in front of me. I could not get up and go away. I did not want to. But I was deathly afraid of what would happen. We took each other's hands, held them, and looked into each other's eyes. His were very sensual, very sexual. His eyes seemed to go into the very depth of my soul. His hands were wonderful and sent shivers down my back. Physically he was everything I had ever wanted in any man. From the moment I touched his hands I began to shake. I could not stop or control the shaking. I was totally turned-on to him. The shaking did not stop. It only got worse. There was no way out. Once again I was faced with the risk of sharing with another minister my sexual attraction and interest in him. It was time for me to get out of the boat and face the terror of opening my inner self to another man, another minister. I decided to tell him why I was shaking.

I do not remember what I said. All I remember is that we kept holding hands and looking into each other's eyes as I poured out my feelings. I shared with him the long struggle with my sexuality and his affect on me. He did not withdraw. He continued the physical contact. He did not reject me, or get up with disgust and look for another partner. He continued to hold my hands and look into my eyes. The terror of coming out had come and gone. The shaking slowly receded. He was genuinely interested in me, a gay man, and a minister. He was not another Rev. Mr. Judas. I remember asking, "Why did you choose me?" He replied, "Because of your ideas."

When we finally stopped holding hands and looked around, we were alone, the rest had gone to lunch. After lunch I went to the First Presbyterian Church and asked if I could play the pipe organ. They had recently purchased a new one, and I did not think I would have a chance to play it. But I did. That certainly helped me get through the rest of the day. Throughout my years in the ministry I had played the pipe organ in moments of great emotional turmoil. Playing the organ that afternoon helped me through the emotional turmoil within and to get a hold of myself.

We spent a lot of time together during the week. This did not go unnoticed by the other participants. One evening, in response to a question from another minister, I informed the group that the

142

young minister and I were going into San Francisco. Several men jokingly accused me of taking an innocent young lamb to be slaughtered. I do not think any of them knew exactly what had happened between the two of us, but they knew something had taken place.

I had met Mr. Wonderful and was falling in love. It was not reciprocal. He offered support and friendship and seemed to be genuinely interested knowing something about homosexuality. He gave no indication of anything more. He did not hesitate to give me a hug. I hoped for more but did not ask for more. I accepted what he gave. It was enough. Our trip to San Francisco was a fun night. He wanted to see something of the gay life, but I did not know San Francisco that well and did not know where to go. As we walked I noticed how many men cruised him, and I pointed them out to him. We finally found someplace where we could stop for a drink. I do not remember what kind of place it was. As long as I was with him, I did not care where we were.

We returned to the conference and often spent our free time together. It was a wonderful week, and I was contented for the first time in a long time. I remembered a conversation with another minister who said that relationships were for a period of time. They had a beginning and an ending and were not always "till death do you part." I understood what he meant. Love relationships do have a beginning and ending. They are not always forever. This relationship of five days was an example of that idea.

Oh, yes, about the workshop on worship. From the beginning something was missing. At first I could not put my finger on it. One afternoon we went to a church in San Francisco which had a reputation for being a leader in contemporary worship. I thought, "Okay, let's see what you have to offer." As I walked in the church, I picked up a couple bulletins from past Sundays to see if they had made any changes in worship. Shortly after arriving we

143

were introduced to a guitar choir of about fourteen or fifteen young people. They were practicing the hymns for the coming Sunday. I was sitting about the third or fourth row from the front and could hardly hear them. If I had started to sing I would have drowned them out. How could they lead congregational singing? Strumming chords on a guitar in a large sanctuary does not lend itself to leading a congregation in singing. As I sat listening to that futility in sound I understood what was missing in the worship.

The theology of many folk hymns was no different from the traditional hymns, and in some cases it was worse. Looking at the bulletins I had picked up, I saw that the service had not really changed. The prayers were the same. The service had been juggled around a bit. Some thee's and thou's had been discarded. Otherwise it was not much different from traditional worship. The service was addressed to the God-up-there. From my perspective they had put new slip covers on the old furniture called worship and called it contemporary worship.

As far as I was concerned playing guitars and singing folk tunes did not really change worship. They had not changed the theology behind worship. For me and the members in Coos Bay, change in worship had come about because of our theological journey. Our worship was an attempt to express the theology, particularly about Jesus, the Christ which we had accepted. "New forms" of worship went beyond guitars and singing folk songs. It was an expression of who we were in Jesus, the Christ.

Following my return, we made some major changes in worship. Some of the members preferred contemporary worship and others the traditional. We decided that the first Sunday of the month would be a contemporary service held in the fellowship hall. We sat around card tables. The service was informal. It began with a few opening verses, followed by hymns chosen by the people. This gave them an opportunity to sing the "good old hymns" I would not use. Not many people asked for them. This was followed by a presentation designed to stimulate discussion. We used some wonderful short films – three to five minutes in length – designed to do just that.

One Sunday I wanted to consider the beginning of the women's liberation movement. I used an animated film with stick figures. It began with a typical service in a Protestant church. The first hymn was "Faith of our Fathers." When the singing ended an Asian woman's voice asked, "What about the mothers and daughters?"

A male voice answered, "In our religion, fathers includes mothers and daughters."

Whenever in the service the words "fathers and sons" were used, the woman would ask, "What about the mothers and daughters."

The answer, "Fathers and sons includes mothers and daughters." The closing hymn was "Rise up, O Men of God."

"I get it," said the woman, "Fathers includes mothers and daughters."

"Yes." replied the man.

In the final scene were two doors, one with a sign "men," the other "women." The door with the sign "men" opened, and the voice of the woman said, "Oh, I guess we are not included after all."

The round tables facilitated discussion. After a time I would stand and ask for comments, statements, or any questions from the various tables. This sharing of thoughts and ideas was our morning prayer, the meeting of persons taking each other seriously. We followed this with a hymn which led to the communion service. Repeating the traditional words of the communion service while holding bread in my hand, I would break it as I turned to the person on my right saying, "This is my body broken for you."

He or she in turn broke the bread and handed it to the person on the right saying, "This is my body broken for you." Following the breaking of the bread, I would take a pitcher of coffee (the common drink of our day) and say, "This is my blood shed for you," as I filled the person's cup. That person did the same to the next person on the right. When the communion service was over many of the people lingered and a second coffee hour followed.

The theology behind this worship form was that "Christ" was present as we shared our thoughts, ideas, and ourselves. An elder was responsible for providing the bread for the communion service. One Sunday I did not check to see if there was bread at each table. After the service had started, I noticed we did not have bread. We had heart-shaped cookies with pink frosting. I thought, "Oh, boy, what do I do with these?" The hymn I had chosen before the communion did not go with heart-shaped, pink cookies. My memory came to the rescue. I recalled an old Gospel hymn which said something to the effect there was a place of quietness near to the heart of God. When we had finished singing, I said, "As the heart of God was broken when Jesus hung on the cross, this cookie represents the heart of God broken for us. Jesus said, 'Do this in remembrance of me.'" I broke the cookie, turned to the person on my right and said, "This is my body broken for you." A closing hymn was sung and the benediction given.

On the second Sunday of the month a traditional service was held in the sanctuary. We followed the order of service in the Book of Common Worship Provisional Services. This service included a sermon and the traditional communion service with the elders serving the elements to the people seated in the pews. This service was intended to meet the needs of those who did not feel comfortable with our contemporary communion service in the fellowship hall. The members were urged to attend both services, thereby giving support for each other's needs. Many members did come to both.

On the third Sunday of the month we held a contemporary service, and I was free to do as I pleased. Well, almost. For me one of the characteristics of contemporary worship was the involvement of the people in the act of worship. Their participation was more than listening to the minister preach. I provided time for them to respond to what I had presented in the sermon. I invented the "Now Lesson." It took the place of either the Old or New Testament reading found in traditional worship. The "Now Lesson" was a message from our world.

One Sunday I explored the use of sound, sight, and emotions in worship. I used the pipe organ for loudness and silence, words for emotions, and sight at the offering. A set of slides entitled "Thanksgiving," flashed on a screen accompanied by the music "Suppertime" from the stage play Snoopy. My son had spent hours looking through Peanuts cartoons for pictures of Snoopy at supper time. He looked for pictures which depicted the incredible joy displayed by Snoopy when his food was brought to him. My son drew those pictures on slides and correlated them with music of "Suppertime." As the record was played, the slides clicked by, and this was our "Prayer of Thanksgiving" as the offering was received.

On the third Sunday I usually gave a short presentation designed to elicit a response from the congregation. The Celebration of The Christian Life on this Sunday emphasized the positive values of the Christian faith, helping us to leave the sanctuary and share our 'love' with others.

The fourth Sunday of the month was a traditional preaching service. I no longer wore my robe, and some Sundays I did not even wear a tie. A turtle neck shirt sufficed. When there was a fifth Sunday, we gathered for breakfast, and the Celebration of the Christian Life could be either traditional or contemporary, depending upon my decision.

The variety and changes in worship did not save us from the coming experience of Good Friday. Our change to different forms of worship was an example of both dying and coming alive and I began to understand that Good Friday was the other side of Easter and before we can get to Easter, we must experience Good Friday. At the same time were experiencing the statement that "Christology equals Anthropology." This means that whatever happened to Jesus would happen to us. Good Friday (death) precedes Easter (rebirth). This was evident in what happened in our Celebration of the Christian Life. No longer did the members sit beside each other, nod, smile, and after the service go home until next week. We were becoming a living organism, people concerned about each other, not only on Sunday morning, but during the week.

From the New Testament point of view, during the experience of the cross we have no control over Easter. We cannot have Jesus hanging on the cross saying to his disciples, "Okay, I'll see you on Sunday." No way! To die in the New Testament sense is to give up all control over what will happen when we come alive. We will come alive in a manner which only time will reveal. Many people say, "Well, I am willing to give up this or that, if I can have this or that. That is bargaining. That is not the meaning of the cross, of dying, Good Friday, or of coming alive, Easter.

In my own life the dying, which had been taking place over the past year, involved my sexuality. I had to die to the idea of appearing to be a straight man, a straight minister. I had to stop living the lie of the past years, so I could come alive as the person I really was. I knew deep within that my sexual orientation would not change how I functioned as a pastor. I was sure not having to live a lie would enable me to be a better pastor. This meant I would have to face the terrors of "coming out of the closet" to the congregation and the community. How soon I did not know.

148

ANOTHER MR. WONDERFUL?

Before I went to the office in the morning I attended my first coffee at a local bakery. The Rev. Mr. Edwards, pastor of one of the important churches in Coos Bay came in with another man and introduced him as his new assistant, Anthony. I smiled and thought, "I hope this one has more life in him than the last one." I did get the impression Anthony was a nice person, the type anyone would like to know. There was no physical attraction, nothing indicating anything other than a professional acquaintance-ship would happen.

Circumstances brought us together in the next couple of weeks. Yes, he did have more life than the last one. He had a disarming smile. I discovered he could be serious and had the same kind of gross humor I did. Anthony was an assistant minister in charge of Christian Education. Too often assistant ministers are called to work in Christian Education with little or no training. This was Anthony's situation. When he discovered I had spent many years in Christian Education, he came for help. I shared with him what I knew, and we developed a wonderful professional ministry. His theological training had exposed him to many of the same ideas I had met in my continuing education. We discovered we were going in the same theological direction.

Our times together often started with chitchat, punctuated with our gross sense of humor concerning "religious matters." Yet, in a flash we could, and did, switch and become very serious. We shared our feelings, ideas, and doubts in regards to what we as ministers were supposed to believe. Up to this point in my ministry, I had noticed the reluctance of ministers to share their theological thinking with one another. Theology, as a subject of conversation, was to be avoided as if it were the plague. Discovering that Anthony enjoyed talking about theological matters was a special treat for me.

I had found a friend, and the friendship grew. Every now and then, when he left, I thought he gave me the same signal I had gotten from the Rev. Mr. Judas, the signal one gay man gives another when in the straight world. When Anthony did that, I would said to myself, "Keep that up Anthony, and I will seduce you." By this time he was more than a friend to me, and I wondered if there might be more on his mind as well.

Shortly after Anthony's arrival, he, the Rev. Mr. Edwards, three other clergymen from Coos Bay, and I began meeting once a month. I referred to us as the Brothers Six. Our agenda? To have lunch and tell slightly off-colored jokes. That was all. No more. This condition was at the request of one of the priests. Great! I would enjoy a meeting which was for fun and not business. It was a time to shed our religious "habits" and become human beings. After several months of meeting, a real fellowship of ministers developed. We began to see the possibility of our churches working together.

The first opportunity came when Anthony was to be ordained. Usually participants in ordinations were kept within the denomination. But the Rev. Mr. Edwards decided to depart from tradition, and the Brothers Six had a part in the ceremony. Most of the ordinations I had attended were rather boring events filled with tradition, but this one would be different. A friend, no, someone who was becoming more than a friend, would be ordained, and I would have the privilege of laying my hand on his head at the proper time in the service. The laying on of hands by those already ordained was the symbol of the authority of the ministry being passed to the one being ordained.

Shortly after New Years one of the Brothers Six gave a party. He provided food and drink. The rest of us took it from there. As the evening progressed, the signals from Anthony became more frequent and more obvious. There was something on his mind

150

other than our friendship. I wondered what it was and said to myself, "Watch it, Anthony, you are getting a bit bold." He was safe. I would not start anything while the others were around. I was the one in danger. At one point I had to go to the bathroom; not knowing Anthony was there, I walked in. He grabbed me and planted a great big kiss on my lips.

To me it was more than just a friendly kiss. I had been right all along. I had not misinterpreted his signals. Now what? This was not the time or place to continue. We agreed to meet in a day or two and talk about that kiss. When we met, I shared with him where I was with my sexuality, and where I wanted to go with it.

After a short conversation, I asked, "Where did you learn those signals you have been giving me?"
    "From a conference I attended on homosexuality," he replied.
    I answered, "Oh, no, not that again," and told him I had gotten the same signals from the Rev. Mr. Judas.
    Anthony related a brief encounter with another man in his past, but it had not been more than touching and hugging.
    After a while I said, "If you are interested in exploring a relationship, so am I. If not, let's drop the whole matter right now."

Our relationship continued following the pattern we had established from the beginning. There was more physical touching when the opportunity presented itself, but nothing more. There did not seem to be any pressure to do more. The friendship was the more important, and when and if the opportunity presented itself, I was sure we would consummate the relationship. We did. It was on my birthday. A nice present. What I had long thought would be an answer to my situation had become a reality. Or so I thought.

Anthony began to withdraw, a subtle indication that all was not

151

well. I had noticed the signs and wondered about them, but the joy of the relationship pushed any fears into the back of my mind. I would become upset when he did not show up as planned or was not in his office when I thought he should be. At least Ed was around, and I laid my frustrations with Anthony on him.

The ministry Anthony and I shared was still there, but Anthony had withdrawn sexually. "Why?" I decided we needed to talk about what was happening, and I asked him to meet me. When we got together it all came out. In essence we decided that we were not ready to divorce our wives, leave our families, and take off to live together in the mountains. Anthony wanted to keep the friendship, but was not interested in the sexuality. "Thanks a whole bunch, " I said to myself. That was not what I wanted to hear.

Understanding my feelings, Anthony suggested we go to "The Ranch." Upon our arrival Anthony suggested I find a stump, take the ax he had brought, and chop away while I screamed and yelled at him. He felt this would help me get rid of my anger "I am not angry at you," I said. "I am hurting, and I am feeling very sorry for myself. Deep within is a terrible ache that does not want to go away. That ache desperately hopes you will change your mind. Hitting a stump with this ax is not going to relieve any of the hurt." For a few moments there was silence. I stood, ax in hand, not moving, just hurting. Looking up, I quietly said, "I will let go. But it will have to be on my terms. Agreed?"

"Agreed."

I did not touch him. I did not dare. I would have broken down. The tears would have been overwhelming and I would have come unglued. I, as a minister, did not dare take the chance of coming unglued. "Let's go." We returned to Coos Bay.

How does a person turn off the deep feelings of love for another person and just be friends? Somehow I would have to find an answer. I knew no person could force another person to love him. Many people try, only to bring great pain and sorrow to both parties. If I could not force myself to give my wife the intimacy and love she needed, I could not force Anthony to love me, no matter how I felt about him. I came up with a plan: nothing clever, nothing underhanded. Just continue having coffee together as usual. I said to myself, "You're kidding. What good would that do?" "Wait and see," I answered.

We continued to have coffee as usual only I made sure we met at a restaurant where there would be little chance of anyone walking in who would know either one of us and join us. The first time we met, Anthony did not seem to be at ease. I did not attempt any physical contact, not even a handshake. I made no sexual innuendoes, no sarcastic remarks about what had happened. I assure you, I could have done that quite well. I tried to keep this first time together as much as possible in the same tenor as we had enjoyed before the big kiss. Sensing I only wanted to chitchat, Anthony began to relax. Slowly the ease of being together, a trademark of our relationship, began to assert itself. I did not know how he felt. He did not say. I did not ask. I know how I felt. He was mine, all mine for the moment. I could afford to be brave, magnanimous, and a bit self-righteous at how mature and adult I was being. It worked.

Sexuality has a lot to do with owning the other person. It has a lot to do with control. It says, "You are mine in a way no one else is, and I am not willing to share what you are to me with anyone else. And as long as we are together I will make sure you do not belong to anyone else, come hell or high water." That is nothing more than controlling the other person in the name of love. As long as we were having coffee and no one else was there, he was all mine. But at the same time, I could not revel at being in control. While I was in control I had to turn off my desire for him to be my lover

My success was a terrible two-edged sword. I was satisfied for the moment, but I knew that when we parted I would no longer be in control.

When it was time to go, we went our separate ways. Then the heartache, the loss, the pain, the loneliness all took over. When I was safe in my car, I yelled, "Damn! Damn!" while hitting the steering wheel, letting out my anger. My anger was not at Anthony. It was at the situation over which I had no control. The ache and the loss were deeper than the anger, and they would take over. I would feel sorry for myself. My old friend depression would set in. If Ed was in his office when I returned, he would get the brunt of my anger and frustration. He understood. He listened patiently and let me fuss and fume.

Time is a great healer if we allow it to be, and after meeting in that manner for some months, I was able to let go of my desire for Anthony as my lover. Our friendship was intact, and in time I could even give him a friendly hug. My love for him and my memory of our love is now safely tucked away where precious memories are kept.

I had been pondering all that had happened between Anthony and myself when that bright light once again flashed in the back of my mind. Being a gay man and appearing in public as if I were like any other man was a lie. Living that lie was difficult and dishonest. Having a love affair with another minister and both of us hiding behind our clerical robes would have been a double lie. I could not live a double lie. I had thought the answer to my situation was to have a clandestine affair with another minister. No way. I had to die to that idea. This affair was both a dying and also the beginning of coming alive. The end of a love relationship was death, but the friendship which continued helped me through the difficult times ahead.

Once again I was confronted with the fact that my gayness was a given. The only choice I had was how I responded. I had followed the standard procedure. Do it in secret. Not an honest response. It missed the mark. It began to sink into my thick skull that I would have to get out of the boat, proclaim I was gay, and face whatever the consequences might be. As to my marriage, the only course of action – divorce. When? I did not know. It would come sooner than I expected.

Meanwhile I managed to continue to function as a pastor. The no-God theologians had incurred the wrath of many ministers in the mainline denominations and, of course, the fundamentalists. A spin-off of the fundamentalists was a group of young people known as "Jesus Freaks." It was well-known throughout the community that I was preaching, "there is no 'God.'" That was what people thought, and in a way it was true. One day a knock on my office door interrupted my thoughts. Looking up I saw two young people. I invited them in. They introduced themselves and identified themselves as "Jesus Freaks." "We have come," began one of them, "because we have heard you preach there is no 'God.'"

I replied, "If you mean the Almighty, All-powerful, God-up-there, then you have heard right."

After I made a short futile attempt to explain what I did believe, one of them said, ""If you do not stop what you are preaching, the judgment of 'God' will come upon you."

I answered, " I have simply rejected an idea of 'God' which is not Biblical. I will take my chances." A few more threats. End of conversation.

This lead me to try another sermon on the doctrine of God. This time I turned to the Gospel of John which does not conceive of God being "up there."

"God is spirit, and those who worship him must worship in spirit and in truth.' (1) We who live in a materialistic world have great difficulty with anything in the 'spiritual' realm. We think the material and spiritual worlds are opposites and that no relationship exists between them. To say, 'God is spirit' means 'God' is not something we can put in a test tube and say, 'See, here He/She is.' Spirit literally means 'breath,' or 'wind.' Wind is something we can experience, but cannot control. 'God' is like the wind: free, not confined, not contained, not able to be possessed, but moving in and through all things. 'God' is experienced, and that is as far as we can go.

"Because we live in a technological world many of us do not feel there is anything in our lives which is not physical. Think again. The emotional forces within us, the value systems of our culture, our families, our social and economic ideas all unconsciously influence what we do day by day. These values are spiritual. They are not something of the material world. Life happens. That is as far as we can go. Perhaps this explains why it is easier to get to the moon than to tackle the problems of poverty, war, disease and overpopulation. We need to remember that when Yahweh breathed into that clay we received a soul which can respond to 'The Spirit' free and moving in and through all situations. That is as far as we can go."

In the coffee hour which followed I heard someone say, "This definition of God is the going one for this week." That about sums up the feeling of those who listened to me week after week. It also shows how nebulous it was and is to seek a new name for "God." I felt good about the person's statement. The advice of Harvey Cox was on the mark. We cannot just come up with a name for "God." When the time comes it will happen. I continued trying to explain what I meant by the word "God," and this meant change. What I felt at any given moment could and did change in the future. In this case it was an attempt to show the meaning of "I Am" and the idea of "God as spirit" were one and the same. That which we call "God" is not being, but spirit.

In another coffee hour someone suggested that our worship on the first Sunday of the month was more like a group therapy session. My first response was that the criticism was valid. But on second thought the criticism was not completely true. One of the hopes of group sessions is that something will happen between the people involved. If we suffer from faulty human relations, then where else can we find help but with other humans? To say our worship had become a group therapy session was close to the truth.

In reading the letters of Paul it becomes evident those people gathered together and became the body of Christ. In their meetings they ate, drank, talked, laughed and their physical, spiritual and mental needs were met. If we could transport ourselves back into history, we would see the gatherings of those early Christians was what we would called a group therapy. They called it 'a love feast.'

I continued with another idea found in the Gospel of John. The writer says that God is "agape." This idea of love is an important perception if we wish to live our human lives to their fullness.

"God is love (agape). In this Jesus of Nazareth, Yahweh who is spirit, love and light, became a reality in a particular human being. The meaning of the Incarnation is that this downward movement of love came into the realm of human life. Think of it. Human life is the only fit vehicle for love, spirit and light. These attributes of human life are not material, but of the Spirit and can be experienced in our lives. They are not automatic, but they are free and can flow

157

from one person to another. But never, never, does this happen without the experience of the cross.

"Love (agape) is not a concept to be debated; it is an experience. Dostoevsky once said that where he saw love in action, he had met God. That is it! It is just that nebulous. If it appears that God is dead in our messed-up world because of the problems of war, poverty, overpopulation, you name it, it is because we have barred 'God's love' from those realms of life where we do our living. Those who insist that the preacher stick to preaching the gospel and leave politics to the politicians are placing boundaries where 'agape' can function. Whenever we insist that 'God' has no right to enter this or that compartment of our lives, we deny love the opportunity to function. By insisting 'God's love' only functions in the sacred, and not in the secular, we make ourselves blind. Christian love (agape) is love with no strings attached. A person's needs are met, not deserved, not earned. Agape is not an equation, so much done, so much received.

"We need to take 'agape' one step further. The writers of the New Testament interpreted Yahweh's love in terms of the Suffering Servant. The idea of Suffering Love is not about self-inflicted pain as a means for the growth of the soul. That is not Biblical. Neither in the Servant passages in the Old Testament, nor in the Suffering Love of Jesus in the New Testament are we talking about self-mutilation, but rather a selfless giving, a willingness to suffer for what is right. The early church looked back on the Servant Passages in the Old Testament and used them to interpret the life of Jesus. In the idea of Suffering Love the early church had found answers to its own situation.

"This raises the question, 'How do we grapple with evil in this world?' One answer is to accept the Suffering Servant who comes in love as a model for human living. Gandhi responded to this. Martin Luther King understood this.

When King led his nonviolent demonstrations, the demonstrations were very violent. But it was the response of white people that was violent, not the demonstrators. There are times in the history of the human race when the only answer to oppression is Suffering Love. It is stronger than all the sources of power which human beings depend upon."

A RAY OF LIGHT

The Brothers Six continued to meet, but we had come to the conclusion that it was time for us to do something other than have lunch and spend an hour or so telling jokes. We decided it was time for the four churches to have a high-powered professor come and give a series of lectures. Professor Neil Hamilton arrived. He talked about The Persistent Agent of Suffering Love which became the next step in my understanding of "God."

"When Hamilton talked about "God" as the Persistent Agent of Suffering Love, he was not talking about a personal God, but about an agent: a person or some event in history in which love, mercy, justice, righteousness were breaking through the confining institutions, organizations, or cultures which kept people in servitude.

"What forces are there in our lives which try to keep us in bondage? Quite simple. They can be a false religious concept of the Christian faith, an economic system, a political system, a social system, or any value system which dehumanizes human beings. They can be any repressive, closed system in any area of life. Along comes the Persistent Agent of Suffering Love, challenging the institution, the system, the closed idea – and out of conflict, pain and suffering new life emerges. We may or may not be able to understand who or what the agent was, but we know from the results the Persistent Agent of Love was involved.

"Traditional emphasis has been upon Christ as Savior and King. There is no lack of hymns attesting to these ideas. The Palestinian Jewish church looked for a triumphant Christ. They were waiting for the Davidic Messiah, a charismatic political leader, who in one massive battle would get the Romans off their backs and subdue the nations of the world. Then the conquered would all have to come to Israel. This did not happen. In fact just the opposite. Those ideas brought about a massive destruction of Jerusalem.

"The Hellenistic Jewish church also thought in terms of a triumphant Christ, at least that part of the early church which had Peter at its head and is found in the Gospel of Mark. The final battle of history was to happen soon, and the church did not have to take any responsibility for that event. But the end of time did not happen. It still has not happened. So it must be that these triumphant, powerful, interpretations of Jesus are not what it is all about.

"If in our terminology we think that which we call 'God' is going to come from above, and with one well-placed hydrogen bomb bring down all the evil arrangements in this world and set up the Kingdom of God, we are mistaken. To change history in this manner is to be trapped into the same kind of thinking as trapped Peter, Jewish apocalyptic thinking, and anyone else who thinks that violence is the way to establish power on this earth. Many have tried and failed.

"'The God' of the scriptures is a much more modest operator than his people have supposed, and than you and I have been taught. We are confronted with the idea of 'God' as the Persistent Agent of Suffering Love, quietly working in and through social and cultural conflicts in which human life is at stake and in and through personal discord. Again, I must say, 'No one can get to the joy of Easter and bypass the crucifixion. Mark in his Gospel tells us to look at the Suffering Jesus. If we are willing to follow that route, then we can participate in whatever resurrection there will be. But Jesus's resurrection cannot be ours. The resurrection witnessed by those in the New Testament cannot be ours. Our own resurrection can only be ours, but not until we have first thought through this bit of suffering with no conditions on what will happen later. We cannot bargain with 'God' on what our resurrection will be. As long as we try to control any aspect of our coming alive it will not come to be. Why? Because we have not really died to our situation."

Another idea I received from Neil Hamilton was that the world makes many promises, but does not fulfill them. He said that he lived in a neighborhood inhabited with a large number of junior executives employed by large companies. He had observed that many of them worked long hours every day, and often on weekends to finish their work. When their assignment was finished and turned in, it was their bosses who took the credit, the financial rewards and the promotion. The junior executives were left empty-handed.

I began to check out that idea and discovered it was true. One realm of life in which this happened was in sports. Coos Bay was fanatic in its support of the high school football team. Since I had attacked many of the sacred doctrines of the institutional church because they were not Biblical, I had no qualms about attacking those institutions in our society where I felt promises were being made, and not fulfilled. Football was one. No longer was it a game which grown men played for their enjoyment. Professional football had become a business and money ruled what happened on the field of play.

When we changed to different forms of worship on Sunday morning, the fifth Sunday was free and open. I felt it was time for me to attack American's Newest Religion – Football. I wanted to point out the conflict between the promises by the sports world, football in particular, and the rewards received by most of those who played it. Raising questions about the value systems of this world was essential in good preaching. With tongue in cheek I prepared a worship service indicating the similarities between worship in many churches, and what happened on the football field. The order of worship was traditional, but not the words.

A FOOTBALL GAME
A RELIGIOUS EXPERIENCE

Pregame Activities	Breakfast
Pregame Music	PRELUDE
Welcome	CALL TO CELEBRATION

LEADER: From East, from West, from North, from South, men, women and children who are Christians have come to celebrate their life together.

PEOPLE: We have come to this celebration out of the experiences of this past week. We have come with different needs, hopes and aspirations to experience this hour together.

LEADER: This is a time to be joyful and to sing. We sing the praises of the life we share with each other bound in Christian love.

PEOPLE: We do not need fine words or solemn faces to sing of our Christian life. All we need is to open our lives and let our joyful songs come forth. This is a time to sing.

Star Spangled Banner	HYMN
Pledge of Allegiance	AFFIRMATION OF FAITH

The New Testament tells us that in Jesus of Nazareth, Yahweh became so lost in human life that ever since all of human life has become "sacred." That same free, expressive, joyful, outgoing love seen in Jesus can be ours as well. If we seek the fullness of our

162

human life, it will be found as we lose our own lives in outgoing concern for others whether we like them or not.

Playing the Game	ELEMENTS OF WORSHIP
Huddle	SCRIPTURE LESSON
Running the play	COMMENTS ON SCRIPTURE
End Run	ANTHEM
Third down-penalty-clipping	CONFESSION OF SIN

Almighty and most merciful Father, we have erred and strayed from thy ways. We have followed the devices of our own lives. We have missed our given assignments. We have left undone those things which we ought to have done, and have done those things which we ought not to have done. We are faced with the judgment of our actions. We recognize we have not lived up to the fullness of our human lives, and this we regret. We look forward to the future in the hope of doing a better job of human living. Amen.

Completed touchdown pass	ASSURANCE OF PARDON
Fans go wild – sing Alma Mater	HYMN
Commercial Time	ANNOUNCEMENTS
Halftime	
Entertainment for the fans	SPECIAL MUSIC
Words in the locker-room	SERMON
Other Scores	CONCERNS OF THE CONGREGATION
Game ends, band plays	CLOSING HYMN, POSTLUDE

In the sermon I raised questions about the claims and value of sports. One is that if a young man is successful on the athletic field he is certain to be successful the rest of his life. Sports builds character, instills discipline, encourages teamwork, all of which will help later in his life. In reality this may or may not happen. About the time I gave that sermon I was shocked to read about the death of the first defensive lineman who had become a hero. He was found dead in his room from an overdose of drugs. His death brought to mind a saying of Jesus, "What will a man gain by winning the world, at the cost of his true self?" (l) But then, what did Jesus know about football? Or what is important for the fulfillment of our human lives. The world makes many promises, but does not deliver.

All cultures have a right of passage from boyhood to manhood. In American culture that is through sports, football and baseball being the top sports in which a boy becomes a man, and proves his manhood. Many men who are physically small spend much of their time looking for a fight with larger men to prove they are not a sissy. Although I am small physically I did not go around looking for a fight with anyone. Since sports as a rite of passage was not open to me, I had to find another way of understanding my manliness. Being gay only compounded the process. Like many others I turned to the scholastic realm. This in itself was not much help because it was only recognized at graduation. It was this theological journey which freed me from the traditional teachings of the church and from my past. Getting out of the boat, trying to function as a Persistent Agent of Suffering Love, helped me accept myself for the person I am. My maleness took second place.

ENDINGS AND BEGINNINGS

Life in the Hannon household had been changing. Our children had grown up. Our daughter was in her senior year, and her brother was a few years behind. They were busy as most high school students are. Parents are important, but are relegated to the background of their children's lives at that age. My daughter had shown considerable talent in the field of art, and my son in music. They were responsible young persons, and we did not have any great problems with them at this time in their lives.

One weekend both of them were gone. It was devastating. There was no sound in the house except the television, if it was on. We did not have anything to say to each other. I am sure most couples would have looked forward to a weekend without their children. In our situation it was not great. For me, it reinforced the decision we had made after our visit to the psychiatrist. When the children got to the right age, we would certainly rethink our marriage. No way would we spend the rest of our lives in such a situation. The idea of a divorce began to become a real possibility.

One bright spot in that year was our daughter's wedding. As parents we did not feel the marriage would work, and we voiced our opinion. It was not accepted. Having done that, we supported our daughter's decision. Much of her life had been involved in the activities of the congregation. They were family to her, and she wanted them to be at the wedding. I had long felt weddings and funerals of church members should be held on Sunday morning as part of the worship service. This was my opportunity to do such a wedding. It would be the main part of the Celebration of the Christian Life, and the coffee hour would be the wedding reception.

The members of the congregation were invited to the wedding. The service became an activity involving many of the members. Our son and the organist prepared a piano and organ duet for the prelude. The choir prepared a special anthem, and one of the members sang a solo. Many close friends in the congregation worked on the reception. I often wondered what the groom's family thought about all of this. They were not church-going people, but took it in stride as the family of the groom was expected to do.

I had been warned by other ministers not to say anything at the wedding. In their experience it was not easy for a father to talk to his daughter in front of a congregation when she was getting married. But then, I did not expound any great words of wisdom at any marriage. What I had to say concerning marriage I said the Sunday before.

"I suggested we compare marriage to a game in which three games are being played simultaneously. Each person has his or her own game to play. But the most important game is the one they play together. Two people come together because, as they contribute to the larger game, they receive intangibles from each other which supplement their growth as individuals and which they would not receive living alone. I suggested that people in a marriage need to give it all they have, and then some. But if in time the marriage became a death trap for either, no longer a source for their growth, then divorce should be considered.

After the wedding they took off to the East Coast where he was in the submarine service. Within six months our daughter had come home. We supported that decision. It was better to admit the mistake as soon as possible, rather than try and keep it going. I knew our children would make some mistakes in their lives. When they did, the door was open for them to return and put their lives back in order. She came home. He got an emergency leave and followed. It was rather messy. I took him out to the ranch, which gave us time to talk. I do not know if I helped. At least he did not make a big scene about the divorce. To my daughter's credit, she did learn from her first mistake, and would marry later. That marriage has lasted through these years.

Some time later there came a knock on my office door. Looking up I saw a young man I felt I should know. He was one of the two men who had come for help seeking a conscientious objector's status with the draft board. His had been rejected. He related some of his experiences in the armed services in Vietnam and then said, "I have another request. I am planning on getting married, but there is a slight hitch. The woman I am going to marry is married. She, her husband, and I have been living together for some time and have decided now is time for the men to change places. Will you perform the wedding service?"

He continued sharing insights about their living together and finished by saying that the three of them had come to the conclusion it was time for them to make this switch. It was the natural thing to do. "Oh, by the way," he added, "we have decided her present husband will give her away to me." I agreed to perform the wedding.

It took place in a cow pasture. Fortunately no cows had used it for some time. The guests formed a circle, with the groom and myself in the middle. The bride, with her arm in the arm of her former husband, walked from the house, entered the circle, and was given by her former husband to be married to this man, his friend. It was a touching wedding, one I have not forgotten.

One of the guests was Ken Kesey. I had a chance to talk with him and shared with him how I had used some of the ideas from his book *One Flew Over the Cuckoo's Nest* in my teaching and preaching. He talked about a new book he was writing, and I felt we were on the same wave length in much of our thinking. After a short visit, I had to leave. My family was waiting for me in Eugene.

Somehow or other I thought I was to meet them at one place and they thought another. It took some time for us to find each other. They were not too pleased with this mix-up. We returned to Coos Bay.

A group of us went out to the ranch for our annual summer picnic. When we arrived it appeared someone was living in our unlivable structure. We wondered who it was. No one showed while we were there. At a later visit, I discovered a transient who had moved in. I thought it was okay for him to be there. He could watch over the place. But my wife and others in our group said he should go. I asked him to leave, and he did.

I stood looking at that house and wondered what to do with it. I decided to burn it down. That would be the best thing to do. As I was pondering this, a neighbor who lived further up the road stopped and asked, "What are you going to do with the house?

I replied, "I am thinking of burning it down."

"If I tear it down, can I have the two-by-fours in it?" asked the man.

"Gladly," I replied. He and I were in for a surprise. The only place he found any two-by-fours was in the roof. The walls consisted of four by four posts at the corners, with two-by-sixes running along the top and bottom of the walls, and boards nailed to the top and bottom two-by-sixes. The inside walls were quarter-inch plywood.

When the neighbors had removed everything they could, the house was still standing. It was not even shaky. They arrived with two four-wheel-drive jeeps, put ropes around the outside of the house and began to pull. It took them over two hours to pull that house down. As I watched them, I thought to myself, "Wait till I see Robert R. and ask him why a person had to use two-by-fours in walls. There were none in that house and it had withstood the snowfall, wind, storms and, for a while, the pull of two jeeps.

Returning to Coos Bay I went to the church and wondered about the changes in the life of the congregation. The members had wrestled with the new ideas of who and what Jesus was, and what those ideas meant to them as individuals and to the congregation. They too were troubled by members who had left the church. It was a time filled with uncertainty. We did not have any well-laid-out plans. No message from above floated down with instructions. It was all in our hands. Well, almost all. We did know we were a group of people with abilities, talents, and the willingness to be "The Christ" as found in the writings of Paul. One of the elders summed it up when he said, "I have been freed from having to come to worship every Sunday because I had to. Now I come because I want to." He had been freed from being religious, to celebrate his faith in the presence of others. And this celebration sent them out into the world to function as Christ to others. It was an experience of having died to the old, and to come alive in a way we had not fashioned.

Still we did not know what the future would be. All we could do was to go out into the world in "agape," which meant being concerned about others with no strings attached.

The word "mission" had always represented something out there somewhere in Asia, Africa, South America, maybe in the big cities, but not in Coos Bay. For the first time in my ministry and in the life of the congregation, "mission" would be in our church building and the community. That meant we needed money to provide us with a focal point from which we could express who and what we were as Christians in Coos Bay, Oregon. The day care was in full swing with a full-time director. That was mission.

This was the time of Angela Davis and her effect on the Presbyterian Church. She was a black woman accused of a crime and put in the county jail in Marin County, California. While she was in prison everyone who came to the county court house was searched. If you were a black woman you were subjected to a complete search. Several members of an integrated Presbyterian church in the county were disturbed by these proceedings. After a while the Session initiated procedures to receive money for her defense. The Board of National Missions of The Presbyterian Church had raised money to be used by Black people, poor people, anyone needing money for legal defense. All proper procedures were followed by the church, and it secured ten thousand dollars for her defense.

There was a fly in the ointment. Angela was a woman, black, and was accused of being a communist. This situation created a monstrous problem within the national Presbyterian Church. Few people outside of the local church believed the account of the situation at the court house, or that the church had followed proper procedure in requesting the loan. The assistance to Davis precipitated the long-festering discontent between the liberal and conservative elements within the Presbyterian Church. For many conservative, influential, well-heeled Presbyterians this action had nothing to do with being Christian. A storm of protest was heard throughout the denomination. The critics insisted the action had little to do with preaching the gospel. To them, preaching "the word" did not include meeting the needs of others.

The reverberations were felt throughout the denomination, and many people felt contributions to the national church would fall drastically. Finally ten black Presbyterian ministers decided to replace the ten thousand dollars. When this information came to light, we in the Coos Bay Presbyterian church considered it. After deliberation, we sent a letter to the Stated Clerk of the General Assembly urging him not to accept this money from the Black constituents. We felt it was an easy out. It gave the national church an opportunity to save face. From our perspective, the denomination had finally done a "Christian" thing. We were one of the few local congregations which did not approve of accepting the money from the Blacks.

The year 1972 seems to have been the final throes of my dying. How dead was I? Quite. There were fewer sermons, partly because two out of the four Sundays I no longer gave a traditional sermon. What I did give were no longer completed. It had been a rule of mine that all sermons were to be finished and typed out by Friday noon. Now all I had were some good beginnings with endings consisting of a few notes scribbled on a piece of paper. I hoped I would be able to finish the sermon without rambling and wasting time. Some of the sermons were filled with my frustrations. This was another preaching no-no. I was still struggling, at a loss, and quite depressed.

I had attacked what had been sacred to the Presbyterians. Calvinist thinking had produced a word image of "God" that was more sacred, more of an idol than any statue in any Roman Catholic church. In the past few years I had been confronted with the vulnerability of my own humanity, my ego. It was frightening. It was something I had not wanted to face. I had to die to all I had considered to be important as a minister and a person. Then I could come into the fullness of my own humanity; a gay minister with many abilities and many weaknesses.

All I can say as I write about these years is, it was hell. Our lives would be much easier if good old hindsight were present when our lives come tumbling in. What has hindsight told me? The life of Jesus as portrayed in the Gospels has to do with the pathway a person has to travel if they wish to find the wholeness and fullness of their life. This is the way to handle that creative conflict which began when Yahweh's breath was breathed into that piece of clay, and we became human beings. Hindsight has taught me the meaning of "anthropology equals Christology." The life of Jesus and the teachings of Jesus are the way to become a full and complete person. But the way to wholeness leads through Gethsemane, Good Friday and Easter. This is the primary model for human life.

One of the most important events in the life of the congregation took place in the fall of 1973. The Session decided the congregation would go on a weekend Planning Retreat. I had done this with the senior high students but never with a whole church. There was a nice camp close to Coos Bay. The retreat

171

would start on Saturday and end on Sunday. If some of the older people did not want to spend the evening, they were urged to attend on Saturday and return on Sunday. A notice was posted on the church door informing any visitors that the members of the church were off on a retreat, and suggesting they attend the Methodist church.

In the quietness of nature, without the pressures of the everyday world, the members could take time to think through the issues we faced. The purpose of the retreat was to see if we could find some answers to the following questions. Where have we been? Where are we going? What is the purpose of this congregation? What goals and objectives do we need to set for the future?

After much give and take we succeeded in writing a theological statement which included what we believed and who we were. (Unfortunately I did not save a copy.) I felt the process of putting down in words what we believed was a more powerful experience for those involved than simply talking. We also set some goals and objectives enabling us to fulfill our statement of belief.

It was a time for rest, relaxation, and getting "to know ya" with plenty of good food. The retreat enabled the members of the congregation to come together in a new way. The schedule was relaxed and there was plenty of time to do as one pleased. Here and there small groups of people spent their free time talking with one another. One man, who was an avid fisherman, had brought his rod and reel to practice fly casting. Soon after he started, others gathered and began to watch. Before he knew it, he was teaching his watchers the art of fly casting. Throughout the weekend we began to become the body of Christ, as far as we were able to experience it.

Dying is a slow quiet process which begins almost unnoticed. Coming alive was also a gradual process and the experience of dying and coming alive at the same time was something we learned from hindsight. There were a few warning signs that something had gone awry in the life of the congregation. We had talked about getting out of the boat, walking on water, crucifixion, and coming alive, and we were beginning to discover these experiences were not confined to the pages of the Bible. They were being experienced in the life of the congregation. Looking back on this I can see the changes were footprints in the sand. We had been lead from a theology in which Jesus did everything for us, to one which said that if anything was going to happen, we would have to be the Persistent Agents of Suffering Love. That meant we could not remain what we had been. Thus the retreat was the beginning of a new life for the congregation.

On "That Sunday" the congregation had been one which came on Sunday morning, sat through a worship service, had a cup of coffee, smiled at one another, waved good-bye, and rushed home for football in the fall, baseball in the spring, and beaches the rest of the time. The retreat was the beginning of the congregation's coming alive, of become a community of persons who felt a responsibility for each other. Now we came together on a Sunday morning to share our concerns with each other and to give encouragement for the issues in our lives. In doing this we found we could go out into the world to meet the needs of others.

THE DIVORCE

In my own life events were beginning to happen which would lead to divorce. Robert R's wife had walked out on the family for about the third time in their marriage. Robert R. felt that was enough. He had been through the same scenario before. Now it was time to do something about it. He told me that the theological journey had given him the courage to take a good look at his marriage, and he had decided a divorce was the answer. I know his wife did not accept his decision, but the divorce did take place, and Robert R. ended up with the children.

His business often required his being away from his family in the evenings. His children were told to call us if they needed any help when their father was away. The calls came, and my wife went to his home in response. Robert R. often came to our house to talk with my wife about the problems he was having with his children. When he arrived I would chat with him for a while, then depart, leaving the two of them alone.

One evening after I had left them, that bright light in the back of my mind came on. An answer to the impossible situation of our marriage: if something happened between the two of them, like falling in love, that would be an answer for all of us. If that did happen I would certainly get a divorce. As time went on I spent less and less time when Robert R. appeared. I became aware that when my wife went to his house in response to a call from one of his children she often would come home later and later. Great! What I had hoped would happen appeared to be happening. It took some of the pressure off of me.

When we purchased "The Ranch" we had a silent partner. He found himself in some financial difficulties which forced us to sell the ranch. With our share of the money we decided to reinvest in another piece of property. One Saturday afternoon Robert R. and our family had spent the afternoon looking at property. We returned to our house, and while my wife was preparing the evening meal, I took Robert R. aside. I told him about our marriage. I told him I was gay, and we had stayed together to give our children a good home. When I finished, there was a moment of silence, and then a big sigh of relief from Robert R. "Well, that makes sense," he said. "I wondered why you were so free with your wife. A few weeks ago, driving home on I-5, I was trying to figure out a way to tell my pastor I was in love with his wife. I

174

was not paying attention to my driving when all of a sudden that curve at Myrtle Creek stared me in the face. I almost went off the highway." We talked about the implications of the situation.

In conclusion I said, "From now on you are responsible for all intimacy with my wife. I will be her husband in public."

I let my wife and Robert R. know that if they wanted to be together twenty-four hours a day I would get a divorce. I hoped they would make the decision soon as the present situation was not that wonderful. A few months later my wife asked me to meet her for lunch. She told me they had decided to get married. I agreed, and we made some tentative plans. I told her I felt it was important that our children know that I was gay. After all, that was the reason behind the divorce. She did not want me to tell them. I replied, "We have not lied to our children and I will not lie about this most important decision." In my own mind I was prepared to accept whatever reaction my children would have; good, bad, indifferent, or even totally rejecting. That was the risk I was willing to take. That was getting out of the boat.

I took my daughter to lunch and told her what was happening with her parents. I also explained that the reason behind the coming divorce was that I was gay. She accepted the explanation and said she could understand how two people of the same sex could love each other. She had noticed Robert R.'s visits and was aware something was up. She felt we could have confided in her sooner than we did.

My son was attending college, and I went to pick him up for the Christmas holidays. Driving from Corvallis to Eugene I told him about the long struggle I had coming to terms with being gay. When I finished I asked, "Do you have any questions?"
    "Is it like I hear in the jokes?" he asked.
    "No," I replied. "You know two gay guys."

175

"I do?" was his surprised response.

"Yes. Ed and Warren," I replied. They had visited us, and my son had not realized they were gay, or lovers. This seemed to help him accept the idea that being gay was okay. We did not talk much more on the way home.

A few days after Christmas I told my wife we needed to have a family meeting. "Our children have something to say to us," I said.

"If they have anything to say," she responded, "They can always come to me."

"No." I replied. "In this case it is our responsibility to hear what they have to say to us."

I insisted on the meeting. A few nights later my family, Robert R., and the man who was going with my daughter sat down to talk about the situation.

A lot of ground was covered in that meeting. The children told Robert R. that he was not their father and would not take my place. They liked him. They accepted him. They agreed with the idea of the divorce, but I was their father. My son mentioned that if I had not told him the reason for the divorce, he would have turned both of us off. It was important that all of those feelings were voiced. We discussed how we would proceed to tell the members of the congregation. I wanted them to hear it from me, and not from the grapevine.

We invited the two families who had been our children's foster grandparents to dinner. After the meal and other niceties, I told them we had decided to get a divorce, and they were the first to know. They were not happy with the announcement, but agreed to support our decision. I asked them not to tell anyone until we had made all the proper arrangements. I assured them I would tell the congregation at the right time.

Next I met with a couple of key members of the Session and broke the news to them. We decided to bring the matter to the Session as soon as possible. A special meeting was called, and I presented the matter to them. I talked about the reasons for the decision, although I did not reveal my gayness at that time. They accepted the reasons given. More important was how to bring this news to the members of the congregation. It was decided I would contact the Presbytery staff member of the Ministerial Relations Division. That was an important first step. Then I would break the news to the minister of the North Bend Presbyterian Church, the nearest Presbyterian congregation to Coos Bay. This way he would hear it from me and not from any gossip. On the last Sunday of January I would tell the members of the congregation.

The Session felt it was important that as many members of the congregation be present as possible. Phone calls were made to the members urging them to be present and informing them that an important matter was to be discussed. That Sunday morning the service proceeded as usual. When it came time for the sermon I said, "I have a sermon prepared, but I could not give it even if I wanted to. There is a matter we must consider. Please move to the fellowship hall, and we will continue there." They left the sanctuary and sat around the tables with an elder at each table. When everyone was seated I said, " We have called you together because I have an important announcement to make. Due to deep psychological differences between us, which we cannot resolve, my wife and I have decided it is time to get a divorce. If you have any questions, ask the elder at your table. After a while we will return, and I will answer any questions you might have." My wife and I left the room.

After a short time we returned, and I answered a few questions. There was a slight pause, then a young man rose and said, "I was afraid when we were called to be here today you were going to announce that you were leaving for another church. I am glad that is not the reason. You have taught us to accept people where they are, and now we must do the same for you." Inwardly I gave a big sigh of relief. I felt the young man's statement had validated the journey the church had taken and my ministry. The question period closed, the service came to an end.

I stood near the entrance of the church so that anyone wishing to express feelings could do so. Most of the members made known their support. But a few told me that divorce was not right for anyone and especially not for a minister. Those people did not return. Robert R. and my wife continued to attend Sunday mornings and sang in the choir as they had done since we had arrived in Coos Bay.

My wife moved out the following Monday. We kissed and she left. Our marriage of twenty-two years had come to an end. It was a strange feeling. The house seemed large and empty, and I felt something was missing. Even though this was what I had wanted, after twenty-two years it was not as easy as I thought it would be. We filed the first joint divorce in Oregon. The state had just passed a law making it possible for people getting a divorce to file a joint request. It was so new the lawyers did not do it right the first time and had to file a second time. I have said many times that the divorce was important, not just for me, but for her as well. She had met a man who could love her as I could not and fulfill her need for intimacy which I had not been able to do.

COMING OUT

The divorce was only the beginning. Now it was time to deal with coming out to the congregation and the community. I was willing to take the risk that, since the members of the congregation and the people in the community had known me all of these years, they would accept my being gay. This was really stepping out of the boat and facing the terrors of life.

Again I planned my approach carefully. From the outside it appeared that I had been dumped by my former wife for Robert R. That was not true and I wanted people to know it was not true. I wanted them to know the reason behind our divorce. I was gay. This meant I would have to come out of the closet. The foster grandparents were the first to know. Next were a couple of key members of the Session. Then I began meeting with a few people at a time. I would share with them the burden of having lived a lie all of those years. When I finished with my explanation I would ask if they had any questions. Usually they did not have any, but I was ready for any they might have had.

For many people this news was the missing piece in the puzzle. Women in particular had sensed there had been something wrong in my marriage relationship, but they could not put a finger on it. Now it all made sense. For most of the men my coming out came as a surprise. They had not suspected I was gay, probably because I was not the stereotype. I was not effeminate. I had played the straight game for a long time, and my interest in sports, the main topic of conversation at the coffee gatherings, had been a good camouflage. Basically I did not appear to be any different than they.

But one group fell apart. It had been in existence before I had arrived on the scene. Robert R., his wife, my former wife, and I had all been part of that group. Having two divorces was more than the group could handle. Part of the breakup was due to several side scenarios which had been going on following Robert R.'s divorce. With the announcement of ours it came to a head at the group's regular meeting. Unfortunately that meeting took place before I was ready to reveal that the reason behind our divorce was my being gay. That was the last meeting of that group, and some of its former members left the church. I was disappointed in the group, but I was not surprised at the results. Perhaps this might have been the blow of death necessary for all.

179

I began to come out to the other adult groups. Many of them were composed of young married couples. Most of them had been to college, had children, and had come to the church because of the theological position. In the discussion following the disclosure of my sexuality no one asked or even hinted about whether or not their boys were safe. I was grateful for that. If they had, I would have asked, "Would you have asked that same question of a straight minister concerning your daughters?" In the 1990's we now know most molestation of children is by straight people and not homosexuals. When I left each group, I would give them a copy of Patricia Warren's book, *The Front Runner*. It was a story of two men. One was a runner and the other his coach. In Coos Bay there was a young man who had the potential of being a runner in the Olympics. It was the right book at the right time and place. I would return a few weeks later and answer any questions they had, no matter how personal. Many of the women related to the love between the two men in the book and understood its validity. Most of the husbands, if they read the book, had no comment.

As more and more people began to know I was gay, the possibility of keeping this a secret went out the window. There was a small coffee group which I attended after tennis each morning. I decided to come out to them. They were not members of the church, but I wanted them to know. Once again, because we had met for coffee and had been open with each other on many subjects, I took the risk they would accept my gayness. They did.

All that was left was to come out to my family. All of them lived in the Midwest or Eastern part of the country. I decided I would write a letter giving them the reason behind my divorce. I do not remember what I wrote, and did not keep a copy. What has remained in my memory was how I felt after I had sent the last letter. I remember great relief.

Now I could be myself. No longer did I have to live a lie. No longer did I have to pretend to be someone I was not. I had finally died to any thought of being straight, and now I could come alive in the fullness of my life, my gay self. I was finally freed to be who I was. I did not have to be on guard every moment.

All of the struggle had taken its toll. I was barely able to keep things going. I was listless and had difficulty in functioning as a pastor. This was evident in my sermons. I was still giving tidbits, and I was not pleased about that. I was wasting much of my time. I needed help. An arrangement was made between the Session and a counselor within the congregation to give me help. In one of our sessions I mentioned that there were several women in the congregation who had been a constant source of irritation and problems. The counselor pointed out that as a gay man I was not responding to the signals they were sending to me. They had controlled their husbands through those signals, but the signals were not having any effect on me; and the women did not know how to handle the situation.

On the other hand, for the first time in my ministry, I felt free to be a pastor. I could relate more openly to people. No longer did I need to keep my distance for fear that in something I said, or did, my deep dark secret would be exposed. Yet, I was not myself. Four years had passed since that disastrous fall of 1970. An elder in the church, one of my strongest supporters, visited me one afternoon. After a bit of chitchat, he reminded me that my preaching had not been what it used to be. I admitted that I was aware of the problem, and like him, had come to realize I needed to do something about it. I said, "I will try to do a better job."

I did return somewhat to what I had done in the past. I completed sermons as I had in the past. Here is a part of my first attempt following his visit:

"This sermon is about men and women's liberation. It is time Christians moved from a literal interpretation of the position of men and women in the Old Testament, from a position of male and female, and move into the realm of persons. Our role in society is determined to a great degree by our sexuality. If we obviously have a male or female body, then we obviously are a man or a woman – in its most simple form, "Me, Tarzan; you, Jane." At the time we are born we receive either blue booties, or pink ones, and we are conditioned to function either as male or female. If male we must function in one manner, and if female in another. The difference between the two is as day and night, as far as the East is from the West. But is the difference between persons only on a sexual level? It is, if we keep it on this level.

"We are beginning to understand that defining our humanness only in terms of our sexuality is to miss the deepest meaning of who and what we are as men or women. In many situations men and women are straightjacketed in their sexual roles. For example, those fathers who might wish to be at home with their children are frustrated by the fact that they must be at full-time 'male' jobs. Men who are not outwardly ambitious or aggressive are seldom rewarded for being gentle, maternal, or emotionally open. Most of the time they are perceived as being weak or henpecked, a perception also held by their wives. Women are often conditioned to prefer a sadistic, wealthy Prince Charming while men often are conditioned to prefer a masochistic, beautiful Cinderella. Both sexes must free themselves and each other from the tyranny of such unreal and destructive images.

"This is what women's liberation is all about. At the same time it is also what men's liberation is all about. Liberation seeks to take us out of the traditional male, female syndrome and into the reality of human beings. It seeks to take us into a life where we are concerned about the kind of person we are in the very depth of ourselves, our souls, our spirits, the essence of who each is as a person. That is not determined by our sexuality only. Long-lasting marriages are built on more than sexuality. If a man and woman come together in marriage simply because they are good in bed with each other, the marriage eventually will come apart. We need to get beyond the sexual and into the realm of persons.

"After the fall, the innocence of Adam and Eve had been shattered and they were ashamed. The love, mercy and kindness of Yahweh was demonstrated in the covering of Adam and Eve with fig leaves. Literally they were given clothing. This is not by chance. If we are this mixture of good and evil, of strengths and weaknesses, then we have control over when and where and to whom we will reveal our inner selves.

"To put this in modern terminology, we are given the opportunity to hide behind masks. This story tells us that we have control over when, where and to whom we will take off our masks. Two people meet. That spark is there between them. As they spend more and more time together, they began to remove the masks. They find their relationship can take the not-so-nice aspects of the other. This is what human life is about, the ability to take off our fig leaves in the presence of others. When we have learned the other will accept us in all of our weaknesses and strengths, we are willing to open ourselves to that other.

"We will find the fullness of our humanity whenever we are willing to take the risk of opening ourselves to another. This dropping of our fig leaves is not done for all people. There are many people with whom we will develop a cordial relationship: the gas station, the clerk at the bank, and many of the service people in this world. We must see them as persons and treat them with the rights and respect due to persons, but we do not wish to get beyond that level. We will not remove our fig leaves for them because the

183

removing is saved for those with whom we want to develop a deep relationship."

Two weeks after that sermon, the following announcement appeared in the bulletin. "On behalf of my children, and myself, it is our pleasure to announce that (my former wife's name) and Robert R. are married. We are happy for them, and it is our hope you will share the same feeling."

And two weeks later, the following: "Lillian Frostad, Phyllis Sullivan, and Velva Waldon invite you to a reception for Mr. & Mrs. Robert R. during the coffee hour."

The sermon was about reconciliation. Here is the essence of what I said:

"We are aware that the love one person has for another can be broken and needs to be mended. But we cannot return the relationship to what it was in the beginning. We are the agents of change, which means that when a relationship has been broken both parties need to work through the problem and develop a new relationship in which both sides will have a chance to grow. Sometimes this means they will be able to stay together and begin a new partnership. But sometimes separation is the only solution for the two people involved. The essence of reconciliation is the beginning of a new relationship in which both persons can continue to grow."

Good Friday had ended for me. Easter was on the horizon.

EASTER

COMING ALIVE

The congregation came alive sooner than I did. Some people expressed the desire to change to another study group. Members were given a chance to do this, but few took the offer. In the beginning the main thrust of the adult study groups had been wrestling with the Biblical material involved in our journey. This had been my responsibility. Now the context in the groups expanded and included social issues, personal growth, and review of books. With this new approach members were able to take the responsibility for presenting the material for discussion and this removed some of the pressure from my shoulders. The strength of the groups varied. A few continued to meet after I left Coos Bay, and one of them is still functioning twenty years later.

Many members had felt a change in the life of the church and began to talk about having experienced a death. There was a feeling of a new reality in the congregation. They felt this change on Sunday mornings and in their group meetings. They had become a living organism. They were concerned about each other and the world in which they lived. This does not mean they were all of one mind, but there was a spirit of belonging, of unity, even while recognizing both their agreements and differences. This was translated into mission.

One of the goals from the church retreat was to establish a Youth Hostel. At the time of the Vietnam War there was great unrest throughout our nation which was manifested itself particularly in the lives of young people. Protests on college campuses, racial riots in our major cities, and everywhere the debate as to whether the Vietnam war was just or unjust: these were symptoms of this unrest. Large numbers of young people took to the highways and byways to see for themselves what their country was all about.

With knapsacks on their backs, they took to walking or riding bicycles. Many Presbyterian parents were concerned about the welfare of their children out on the road. A plan was devised to establish a network of youth hostels in Presbyterian churches throughout the nation to meet this need. The program never reached its dream, but the Youth Hostel in Coos Bay became world famous.

The Pacific Coast and the Western part of our country were natural attractions for the wandering young people. We were the right congregation, in the right place, at the right time. The hostel was named "The Sea Gull." Our church had a large basement with several small rooms. People on the road usually carried sleeping bags, and we felt they could sleep on the floor. If someone arrived who did not have a sleeping bag, we provided a mattress. We installed a shower in one of the bathrooms. The hostel opened at 4 p.m. It offered people on the road a place to stay, a shower, and an evening's meal. We asked for a contribution of one dollar. Guests were limited to one evening unless they requested to stay a second and were granted this by the director. The hostel opened its door in mid-June and ran to Labor Day. In that period of time we served around twelve hundred people. A seminary student was hired to direct the program with funds provided by the Presbytery.

Some of the other churches in the community were also involved. They supplied food, materials, and other miscellaneous physical needs. A couple of the grocery stores contributed food which was still good to eat but could not be sold. Even the police cooperated. If they found someone hiking late at night, they would bring them to the hostel. Members of the various congregations were invited to bring dessert and rolls for the evening meal and to stay and eat with the people at the hostel. Many of us learned to look beyond the beards, long hair, and shabby dress. Underneath the outward appearance was a person worth meeting.

186

People of all ages came, but about one-third were young people from the United State and another third were young people from Europe. The final third included older people, a few runaways from home, and others who did not fit any category. One evening a young man arrived from Germany. He noticed we had a pipe organ and commented about it. I invited him to sit down and play. He did, and gave a wonderful concert enjoyed by the other guests. We did not have many people who gave us trouble. Most of them were very appreciative of what we offered.

During the evening meal an attempt was made to have the visitors share something of where they had been, where they were going, and why they were on the road. Sometimes this lead to a good exchange of ideas, and at other times the discussion did not get off the ground. If they asked why we had the hostel, we would share our thinking that being Christian meant meeting the needs of others with no strings attached. Since they were on the road and in need of a place to stay, something to eat, and a shower, we sought to meet those needs.

After the first year's operation, young people from Europe told us their friends had told them to be sure and visit The Sea Gull in Coos Bay. There was no other hostel like it. Even though hostels were found throughout Europe and Canada, the one in Coos Bay stood out from the rest.

It was the personal touch which made the difference. We received the following letter from a person who had visited the hostel in the first year. "My faith in mankind was once again renewed. Yet, even that wasn't what stole my heart. It was the people at Coos Bay. Everyone who came to the hostel was greeted openly and warmly. They weren't 'loved' conditionally – rather it was because they were simple people. But love was expressed through the meal, the showers, the building, and the lives of the people."

187

During the summer months our Celebration of the Christian Life was on Wednesday evenings and was preceded by a pot-luck dinner. The people who had come to the hostel were our guests. Following the meal we extended an invitation to them to join us in our Celebration without any pressure to attend. Few if any accepted. We did not mind. It was their choice. The program lasted several years after I had left Coos Bay; it continued until the number of people on the road no longer warranted its continuation.

My own coming alive was a slow process. After twenty-two years of married life I was single. I had to learn how to live alone and not be lonely. I had to learn what it meant to be a gay man. Slowly I established a rhythm in my life. I continued to come out to people in the congregation and to some people in the community. This began a pattern which I have followed ever since. If someone is important to me, I want them to know I am gay. Having decided to come out of the closet, I would not and will not go back in.

In my reading I had come across an interesting discovery concerning the human brain. The idea of the brain having two distinct centers which influence how we live made a lot of sense to me, and I shared the ideas with the members:

"Research has indicated that the human mind has two centers of influence. The left hemisphere is connected to the right side of the body. Its predominant activity is analytic, logical thinking, especially as experienced in verbal and mathematical functions. This side seems to take information which comes to us and puts it into a logical awareness. It understands information in a linear manner. Language and mathematics depend predominately on linear time. This is the primary activity of the left side of the brain. It is also the seat of manipulative skills and enables us to understand and master our world physically, verbally, and

188

analytically. Much of our ability to survive depends on this side of the brain.

"An over-dependence on the left hemisphere leads us to perceive ourselves as separated from each other and not related to one another. The more successful we are in manipulating the world and bringing it under control, the less aware we are of our responsibility for it. We have turned the Biblical concept of human life around. In both the Old and New Testaments what happened to people was more important than what happened to their property or material possessions. Our society has it backwards; property and material possessions have become primary and persons secondary. This approach has put us in a quandary. If we are to succeed in this world we must make use of this side of the brain, but it leaves our world meaningless, unrelated, and open to falling apart because there is no center.

"The other side of the brain is the right hemisphere, which governs the left side of the body. It seems to specialize in experience and in intuition. Its ability to verbalize is limited. The primary responsibility of this side is to give us some kind of orientation in space. It also accounts for artistic endeavor, crafts, body language, and the recognition of faces. It takes information which comes to us, diffuses it, and attempts to put it in some kind of relationship. This side of the brain is the source of intuitive capacity and has the ability to make some sense out of the total environment. It appears this side has the ability to discern meaning, to feel supported and upheld by life rather than being constrained to a perpetual struggle for survival. It has the ability to make sense out of our surroundings and enables us to have a context for our existence.

"It is in this side of the brain wherein the religious experience takes place, but any experience is diffused, felt and experienced. Since this is not the logical side of the brain, it often defies a clear-cut word to define it. This

189

means we have difficulty putting into words the meaning of any experience we have. It often seems to defy all of the logic which we have learned to be so important to our existence in our world.

"The religious experience is just that, an experience in the right side of the brain. Therefore, it is difficult to put the experience into words, into logical sentences. It is therefore difficult to share with others. This should not surprise us. 'Yahweh" is verb, and that means we can experience 'I Am' who is in and behind all in this world and universe. But when it comes to trying to communicate this experience to others, we have great difficulty. In reality the important parts of the Biblical material are attempts of the writers to put their experience into words, hoping that when a person reads their words they will have a similar experience.

"This understanding of the brain is not a matter of dividing the brain. Both sides are there and need to be used, strengthened, and supported. Together they enable us to become whole persons. Look at it from the matter of two persons meeting and coming together. Touching someone can be physical, which is a concrete-enough reality, but touching can also lead to an emotional response. The body is simply the physical equipment we have to express our inner selves. I suggest that the body represents the left side of the brain while our 'soul' represents the right side of the brain. Together they make us total, whole human beings.

"What is real in human life? It is not just what we can verify in the laboratory. Jesus reminded the people of his day to look within themselves, and there they would find the Spirit of Yahweh at work even as they saw it working in his life. We are no different. The reality of life is not just in the material world, it is within, where the Spirit of the Divine dwells. We can come in contact with that Spirit, which enables us to respond constructively to those things which happen to us."

Understanding the function of the right hemisphere which receives information which comes to us, diffuses it, and puts it in some kind of relationship helped me understand my long attraction for men. This helped me understand that beginning with Tim my attraction for men was felt, not understood. Since the right hemisphere kept insisting I liked men, and the left side was insisting I was like other men, it took time for me to sort out my experiences and feelings. This understanding of the function of the right side of the mind enabled me to know who I was and I became a whole, complete person. I could accept myself, and peace settled within. This new understanding did not solve all of the problems I would face. Being gay in a straight world does not allow one the joy of being totally relaxed and at one with this world in which we live. But I was at peace with myself, with "I Am," and that is what counts.

SOME THOUGHTS FROM THE GOSPEL OF JOHN

My life was more together than it had ever been, and this was reflected in my work. I was becoming a better pastor. The more I came out to members of the congregation, the freer I became. No longer did I have to watch every movement I made, every word I uttered, for fear of being discovered. I could afford to be a bit more open and congenial with people. I could relax; the big secret was known to many of the members, and that was very freeing for me. Once again I was giving sermons which had been thought through and were completed before Sunday morning. There was another big difference. Most of the theological material through-out the journey had been received from my continuing education and the visit of Neill Hamilton to Coos Bay. These ideas had become internalized over the years and had become part of my life. All of this was preparation for what was to follow. I turned to the Gospel of John which reflected the intense struggle and growth which had taken place within my own life.

All scholars have recognized that the Gospel of John is different from the other three. Who wrote this Gospel is a complicated matter which I will leave to the scholars. It was written long after Jesus died by someone who did not know Jesus in the flesh, but he wanted others to know what he had experienced. What is important is the difference of this Gospel from the other three. It is very spiritual. This means the historical events are subservient to the spiritual or theological understanding of the event. Since it is the Easter event which gives meaning to the life of Jesus who is the Christ, I began with Easter.

"Would it help us to meet Jesus in the flesh? I have a sneaking suspicion many people would nod their heads and say, 'Yes.' But I am not sure this response is true. What would Jesus do if he were alive? Lead an army? Become a king, president, prime minister of an organization which controlled all of the world? Would he have a daily or weekly television program we watch, and if we needed physical healing, or help of any kind, would we place our hands on the television set as he said a few words? I am not sure that, if Jesus did come back, we would even recognize him.

"The first appearance of the risen Jesus in this Gospel was to Mary. She had gone to the tomb and found it empty. She ran back to Jerusalem and told the disciples. They all raced back to the tomb, saw it was empty, and then returned to Jerusalem. But Mary remained. Jesus appeared to her, but she did not recognize him. She thought he was the gardener. Whatever appearance the risen Jesus had, he was not recognizable. After a short conversation Jesus called Mary by her name; then her eyes were opened and she recognized him. The Greek word indicates she was hugging him, and Jesus forbade her to continue to do this. There were more important matters which needed to be done, and she was sent back to the disciples.

"That evening the disciples, with the exception of

Thomas, were gathered together. Jesus appeared and said, 'Peace be with you!,' and showed them his side and hands. When they saw this physical evidence of his identity, they were overjoyed. Thomas was not present at this first appearance, and when he joined the disciples later he did not accept the good news that Jesus had risen. 'Unless I see the mark of the nails in his hand, unless I put my finger into the place where the nails were, and my hand into his side, I will not believe it.' (1) One week later Jesus appeared and gave Thomas the opportunity of touching him, but the account does not say he did. Instead Thomas replied, 'My Lord, and My God.' Jesus said, 'Because you have seen me, you have found faith. 'Happy are they who never saw me and yet have found faith.' (2)

"The great affirmation of this Gospel is that faith is not dependent on seeing Jesus in the flesh. In this Gospel the words and the incidents are symbols revealing the nature of "I Am' as seen in Jesus. The hope of the author was that in reading about Jesus, the Christ, a person would respond and seek the potential of their humanness. Response to the word produces understanding which generates a new life.

"The movement in this gospel is about "I Am" becoming flesh in the person of Jesus. This is Yahweh in human terms. We might say the God-up-there is now the God-in-our-midst, and all who accept this movement, who yield their allegiance to 'I Am,' can become the children of 'I am.' Jesus says, 'If you dwell within the revelation I have brought, you are indeed my disciples; you shall know the truth, and the truth will set you free. (3) In other words, this movement was not limited to Jesus; it happens in the life of anyone who accepts this movement of 'I Am' into the realm of human life.

"But such an idea seems too good to be true because we do not really want it to be true. We do not want that kind of responsibility for our own lives or for anyone else. We would much rather have Jesus in the flesh leading a parade, or an army, or being king or president. It really is very nice to have Jesus back there in history going through Gethsemane, the crucifixion, and Easter for our benefit. It is even nicer to have Jesus off somewhere with the promise that sometime in the future he will return again and make everything right.

"The Gospel of John is more than just words. It is more than writing a story about Jesus. This writer alone, of all the writers in the New Testament, has Jesus saying, 'I Am.' You will not find the 'I Am's' in the other gospels, or in the writings of Paul. Experts in the field of comparative religion point out that the phrase, 'I Am' is not found in any other major religion in the world. When you consider the 'I Am's' notice that they cover all of the necessary ingredients in any person's life. They are also the chief ingredients in relating to others. To have these ideas at the center of our lives is to experience the fullness of our humanity.

"The writer illustrates how 'I Am' was revealed in the events and conflicts which Jesus encountered in his life. Jesus fed a large crowd of people and used the occasion to say, 'I am the bread of life.' (4) Jesus met a man blind from his birth and gave him sight. This caused a controversy among those who witnessed this and finally Jesus said, 'While I am in the world I am the light of the world.' (5) He used the symbol of the door and the shepherd to proclaim that the way to the fullness of our humanity would be found through him.

"The next incident concerns his friend, Lazarus. When informed that Lazarus was sick, Jesus waited a few days before going to his friend. Jesus told his disciples that Lazarus was sleeping and they think he is dead. But the word 'dead' really means 'a finishing, or an end.' Lazarus was not physically dead, but his life had become so disintegrated that he had become one of the living dead. Jesus called, and

Lazarus came forth bound by whatever personal problems which had caused him to become so disintegrated that he did not have a viable human life. Jesus returned Lazarus to an integrated, whole and complete person. This new life was called 'eternal life.'

"This lead Jesus to say, 'I am the resurrection and the life.' This statement is in the present tense not the future. The institutional churches have changed the verb from the present tense to the future. But the writer of this Gospel asserts that 'resurrection' is being rescued from a dysfunctional life into a life that is characterized as eternal. It is a life in which we experienced the fullness and wholeness of our humanness. Eternal life is not the reward of virtue, it is the life of virtue in the here and now.

"In the farewell discourses given to the disciples at the Last Supper Jesus says, 'I am the way, the truth, and life.' (6), and ends by saying these are possible because he is 'The Vine' and anyone who dwells in him will be the branches bringing forth much fruit. I started with the first appearance of Jesus to his disciples following his crucifixion, and I close this short study with his final appearance to his disciples.

"Jesus offered us his peace. The promise was not automatic, but Jesus said that if his words were within the very depth of our lives, if we were tied to him, then despite the hassles of this world we would know his peace. Peace comes within us because our attention is not on the accumulation of worldly possessions or the satisfaction of our desires, but on serving others. Even in the midst of all of the pain, suffering, difficulties, and troubles, there is a peace, a calmness, an inner resource for life which enables us to handle all of the difficulties which come to us. We have assurance that nothing can separate us from this movement of "I Am' into the human situation.

A kind of peace had settled within the life of the church. Many were concerned about social issues, and the church building had become the home base for meeting some of the social needs of our community. The youth hostel was functioning at its best. We had two young people who functioned as the director and assistant director and were very good at greeting the people who came to the hostel.

In some of the adult study groups a fellowship of believers was being developed which would last for many years after I left. The program of the congregation had changed from the traditional to one in which adults and children worked together. Our approach to Christmas had changed, and for several years we gathered at the beginning of Advent for a pot-luck dinner and then a grand decorating of the Christmas tree. We made the decorations after the meal. Adults whose families were gone were also present, and they often came with very special and interesting kinds of decorations. Children were free to wander from table to table and make decorations which appealed to them. All decorations were hung on the tree, and I noticed that, during the coffee hours on Sundays, young children would point out their contribution to others.

In my own life there was a peace which had settled within. No longer having to fear that my great secret would leak out, I could begin to be myself and learn what it meant to be a homosexual. I must admit I did not do this very well. Like many people when they first experience freedom, there was a temptation to more or less throw the restrictions of the past away. Once I was freed from the marriage, I spent a lot of energy on finding Mr. Wonderful. I began several relationships with men, and after a short time their Mr. Wonderful would appear, and it wouldn't be me; I would be left holding the bag.

This did not deter my optimism. I understood that, since I did not respond to everyone's invitation, if others responded negatively to my invitation, that was their prerogative. The search did teach me patience and understanding. It certainly taught me how to deal with rejection. If someone turned me down I would remind myself that Jesus did not promise that we would be free from difficulties. Such an encounter was not the end of the world, and my inner peace was intact. This peace came from knowing myself and trying to meet the needs of the other person, even in a sexual encounter. At this point in my life I was looking beyond the present to the future in any encounter.

THE FINAL DAYS

As the Civil Rights movement came to a close, the gay rights movement began. Although it was centered in the large cities, it gave strength to those of us living in small communities. We did not march in Coos Bay, but thanks to television we knew we were not alone. I often wondered what reaction the people of Coos County would have had if all the gays and lesbians had stood up at one time and flipped their wrists. I am sure the inhabitants would have been surprised at how many of us there were. As time passed, I learned that other gays and lesbians had been watching me as I came out. Some found the courage to follow suit, and others played it safe and remained in their closets.

In the back of the book, *The Homosexual in America*, there is a list of novels and dramas in which homosexuality was a part of the story. Through the years I had looked for these sources. One day I found James Barr's *Quatrefoil*. It was a wonderful book which gave me much encouragement. It is an excellent book about what it was like to be a homosexual in the forties and fifties. I could relate to much in the book because I had lived in those years. I was constantly on the lookout for any material which discussed homosexuality. In the beginning of the seventies, here and there in religious magazines, a few articles refuting the traditional inter-

197

pretation of the Biblical material began to appear. The articles did not condemn homosexuality as the institutional church had done. I collected them and in time I had a large file. One of the better magazines was published by the Presbyterian church and it devoted one issue to a discussion of homosexuality. The various articles in that magazine covered the most aspects of the issue. I would not expect the fundamentalists to consider that material. It was sad that ministers in the Presbyterian church and the other mainline churches did not and still do not use what has been written.

On the first Sunday in May 1977 I had taken some items from the National Lampoon Magazine which poked fun at the traditional idea of the God-up-there and compared them with the prologue from the Gospel of John. During the time of sharing, which followed the discussion, an elder asked, "Shall we talk about your homosexuality?"

I responded, "No, we will not." There was nothing in the material which would have prompted such a discussion. But the elder insisted we talk about my homosexuality. I continued to refuse, and the time for sharing became rather nasty. Calmer heads prevailed and brought a rather bad scene to a close. I was not willing to talk about it at that time because there were a few older women and some prospective new members who did not know I was gay. The Session had already decided that I would give a sermon on the Biblical passages on homosexuality, but I had not decided on a time. As a member of the Session, the elder who had raised all the fuss knew of that decision. I never did know what he had in mind in raising the issue.

Two weeks later, on May 15, 1977 I gave the following sermon:

"As we begin to look at what the Bible has to say about homosexuality, it is important to understand I am not in the proof texting game. If I play that game, I can make Psalm

14 say, 'There is no God.' I can take the third chapter of First Peter and make it say that all of the women here this morning should not be wearing clothes. That is the kind of game the Fundies and conservatives play when it comes to homosexuality and the Bible. I want to examine those passages most used by the fundamentalists against homosexuals. Putting them in their context will enable us to understand what the writers had in mind.

"Nowhere does the Bible say anything about homosexuality as a sexual orientation. Awareness of homosexuality as a psychic orientation is a relatively recent understanding. The Biblical writers were speaking about homosexual acts undertaken by those persons whom the authors presumed to be heterosexual in orientation.

"The story of Sodom in the Old Testament is one passage most often used to condemn homosexuality. Modern Biblical studies have shown conclusively that the major theme of the story has to do with inhospitality and injustice. Those were the sins of Sodom. We are dealing with the extended family, or at least the small city state. In either case you had a small number of people who knew each other and were tied together by the bonds of the clan. They were fiercely loyal to each other. Any stranger was suspect, and Lot was a stranger in that city. To make matters worse, Lot was visited by more strangers, and according to the customs of Lot and Abraham, it was imperative that Lot invite them into his home for the evening and provide them with food and shelter. The writer is trying to show the difference between Lot (Israel) and his adopted neighbors. Lot offers the right and proper hospitality to the strangers, while the citizens of Sodom wished to do them harm. We also need to remember that Sodom had been an extremely wicked city even before Lot arrived. What that wickedness was, had not been stated.

"Other Old Testament writers understood the story of

199

Sodom as a symbol of the utter destruction which the gods would visit upon any city that was so wicked. The Old Testament writers interpreted the sin of Sodom as inhospitality and pride. For instance, Ezekiel writes, 'Behold, this was the sin of your sister Sodom; she and her daughters lived in pride, plenty and thoughtless ease; they supported not the poor and needy; they grew haughty, and committed abomination before me; so I swept them away as you have seen.' (1) In the book of Judges we have a similar incident, only in this case it was a woman who was threatened, the concubine of a Levite. She was released to the citizens of the area, and they so misused her sexually that she was found dead in the morning. (2) We are dealing with two concepts, the absolute sacredness of the guest and the dignity of the male sex. Perhaps we can understand the dignity of men in the Old Testament, but it is difficult to understand that the honor and the life of the women of the family were regarded as expendable. Yet this is what was behind Lot's offering his daughters to the men of Sodom. Whatever sexuality is involved in the story of Sodom, it is not primary. Not until much later, and then from writers outside of the Old Testament, did the sin of Sodom become homosexual. Even then, it was homosexual rape, and rape is condemned utterly.

"Given the statements by other Old Testament writers and the statement by Jesus in Luke (3) that the sin of Sodom was pride and inhospitality, we can assume that the sin was not sexual as was taught later. John McNeil in his book, *The Church and the Homosexual*, has pointed out that the use of the Sodom story in the Christian West may well be one of the ironies of history. In the name of the Biblical account, where the major theme is the sin of inhospitality and injustice, countless thousands of homosexual oriented persons have been subjected to precisely that kind of sin – injustice, rejection, threats.

"The other Old Testament passage frequently used against homosexuals comes from what is known as the Holiness Code. (4) In this code we are dealing with how Israel would worship Yahweh. The nations around her had human sexual practices as part of their worship. Both male and female sexual rites were held, and they were both heterosexual and homosexual in nature and action. Sexuality was seen as a mysterious sacred power through which the participant's life was enhanced. But as far as Israel was concerned, Yahweh was a God who worked to free human lives from slavery through the means of history and not through the cycles of biological life. Therefore, as Israel set up her form of worship it was not to include sacred prostitution.

"If the fundamentalists are going to pick out this section of the Holiness code and apply it to homosexuals, then they must also apply the rest of that code to themselves. Much of the Holiness Code has to do with the forbidding of the lending of money and the charging of interest. Think of what obedience to the code would do to our financial institutions and religious organizations. Since Yahweh owned the land, every seven years the land was to be redistributed. This would prevent anyone from getting rich at the expense of others. Since no one is suggesting we apply the holiness code to our economic system, then we cannot take a few verses from this code and apply them to homosexuals.

"I have another suggestion. If we are dealing with the extended family at this point in Israel's history, then let us keep in mind that anything which threatened the extended family was a 'No-No,' in our language, a taboo in theirs Since homosexuals cannot reproduce their own, such activity was a threat to the family. There is nothing said about females in a homosexual relationship. Taking the idea that whatever threatens the human race is a 'No-No,' and if one

201

of the basic problems of our time is overpopulation, then within the homosexual community we have a built-in safeguard and we ought to encourage it. But perhaps that is asking a little too much, too soon.

"In the New Testament a few passages in Paul's letters have been used as proof positive against homosexuals. The fundamentalists are wrong again. The primary passage is found in Paul's letter to the church at Rome. (5) Paul is talking about men and women changing their natural sexual desires for unnatural ones. He is talking about heterosexuals who are indulging in homosexual activity. It is the heterosexual who is going against his or her nature by engaging in homosexual sex and not the homosexual whose orientation is for the same gender. This passage is dealing with lust which puts the activity in the realm of using the other person for one's own satisfaction and not in the realm of love.

"Paul also wrote, 'There is no such thing as Jew and Greek, slave and freeman, male and female; for you are all one in Christ Jesus. (6) There you have it! All distinctions have been wiped out in Christ, and for me that includes a person's sexual orientation. What counts is the kind of person I am, not my sexual orientation. If I am loving, kind, forgiving, and concerned about others, it is not because of my sexual orientation; it is because that is the kind of person I am, and that is what gives meaning to my sexuality. The question we need to ask is, 'Will my sexual behavior serve and enhance rather than inhibit, damage, or destroy the realization of my humanness?' We are talking about commitment, trust, tenderness, and respect for the other person and the desire for an ongoing and responsible communion with the other. We are talking about the meaning of any particular sexual act within the total context of the persons involved, in the context of what 'I Am' desires for human life. It is an ethic equally appropriate for both

202

homosexual and heterosexual Christians. There is no double standard."

If I were to deliver this sermon today, I would add the following: "What did Jesus, the Christ, say about homosexuality? The pages are blank, and we should leave it there. If not, read again the prologue in the Gospel of John,

> "In the beginning was the Word. . .
> The Word was the true light
> that enlightens all men (human beings);
> and he was coming into the world.
>
> He came to his own domain
> and his own people did not accept him.
> **But to all who did accept him**
> **he gave power to become children of God**," (7)

Notice, there are no exceptions, no exclusions, no brackets.
It says, "to all."

After giving that sermon I attended a hearing of the General Assembly's Task Force which had been given the job of making a recommendation on whether or not the Presbyterian Church should ordain homosexuals. In good Presbyterian fashion the Task Force had done its job very well. They had consulted the experts in all the related fields, considered what they had to say, argued among themselves, and were ready to write a position paper. But before they did that, they decided to take the process one step further. They set up hearings throughout the country which any Presbyterian could attend to voice an opinion about whether or not the church should ordain lesbians and gays.

I went to San Francisco where one of the hearings was being held. I appeared before the committee and asked for the opportunity to be heard. I was scheduled to testify on the second day. I was sure by the time I would testify, my story would be old hat. Boy, was I wrong! I had attended the first day and listened. All I heard was the "righteous right" within the Presbyterian church in California telling – not asking, not suggesting, but telling – us gays and lesbians to repent of our sin and go to a psychiatrist and get cured. Then they would welcome us back into the church. I had tried that, and it had not worked. They really did not know what they were talking about.

The next day I appeared to give my testimony. I could have testified privately before the committee. I refused. Having come out of the closet, I would not return to the closet in order to testify. I also knew that my time as pastor in Coos Bay was coming to an end. In light of what I had heard from the "righteous right," I figured getting another church might be rather difficult. I sat in a chair facing the committee very much aware of the presence of the "righteous right" as I presented my case for ordaining homosexuals. I was armed with a statement of support from the Session of the Coos Bay Church, letters from straight people in Coos Bay, and a brief statement of my own struggle. When I had finished, I answered questions from the committee members. There was a time limit on any person's presentation. When my time was up, a young man on the committee asked that the time be extended. He felt my testimony was unusual and warranted the extended time. The extension was granted, and I continued to answer questions. Since this Task Force represented the whole Presbyterian church, in reality, I had come out to the Presbyterian church.

Later that day I had the opportunity to meet with the young man who had asked for an extension of time. He was a seminary student and an openly gay man. We talked for a short time. He told me I was the only minister to come out to the committee. The seminary student said that he would try to convince the committee or at least a part of the committee to come to Coos Bay and observe my work there. He was not successful. As I write this, that student is still not ordained. A few years before I began this book I learned that another member on the committee, a minister, was also gay. He had kept his secret throughout the hearings and never came out. What a pity!

I returned to Coos Bay aware that my time as pastor was coming to an end. On June 29, 1977 I celebrated the twenty-fifth anniversary of my ordination. A few weeks later I asked the core members of the church to meet with me. Although I had decided it was time for me to leave, I wanted to see if they would concur. When all were present I asked, "Is it time for me to leave?" That really threw them, and they were quick to say, "No." Knowing this would be their first response, I continued to raise other issues. After much agonizing, they finally agreed this was the best for me, and for the congregation. I told them I had already come to that decision. It was decided my final Sunday would be the last one in September of 1977. A reception was held following the service. My ministry in Coos Bay had come to an end.

EPILOGUE

The memories had faded away. Reality returned and I was sitting in my car in the parking lot of the church in Coos Bay looking at the entrance. The years had passed. I went to the door which was open and I decided to go in. The colors from the rose window greeted me and bathed me with their hues. That change had been for the good. I went into the sanctuary and looked around. The pews were facing the front, but they were on an angle pointing to the center aisle. There were a few people around I did not know. I went up to the organ, sat down, and played a favorite hymn. Yes, it was and still is a marvelous instrument. But it was time for me to go to the home of my host.

In my Christmas letter of 1990 I commented that I had started to write the book about my ministry, and if any wanted to share what the journey had meant to them, I would appreciate their comments. I received the following letter:

"I first met Howard Hannon when I went to visit my wife working at the Day Care Center in Coos Bay, Oregon, where we had ended up when we left Boston. I walked in, and this balding fellow in a suit walked up and gave me a marvelous scowl and asked what I was doing there. I got the feeling he wasn't very friendly. I later found out that Howard was quite upset at weirdoes wandering into the church, and he assumed that I was one. I certainly looked the part. Coos Bay at the time was not exactly full of hippies with long hair and beards. I later shaved the beard when someone told me I could never get a job in Coos Bay with a beard, because everybody would assume I was gay and was going to molest children.

"Anyway, I ended up getting a job in the same day care center as my wife, and from time to time had contact with Howard and eventually joined one of the discussion groups in the church. The more I became involved with the discussion groups, the more amazed I was with the stunt that Howard was pulling off of having the whole church divided into discussion groups. It was quite amazing. In fact some of the discussion groups are still running. He certainly knew how to get things going.

"But on to the particular moment. As time went on, Howard's life seem to be falling apart. His wife left, married one of the pillars of the church, and they both kept working in the church. Howard seemed fairly unflappable and told everyone not to blame his wife. I began to think that Howard had a severe Jesus complex; being unwilling to think bad of other people. Because it seemed to me that leaving your husband and going to live with the leading elder was just a little weird. Nonetheless, thinking these thoughts I one day confronted Howard in his office and told him he had a Jesus complex and that he should get mad and jump up and down and yell and scream, and he would feel a lot better. Howard sat at his desk, looked at me for one minute in silence, gave a strange smile, and said to me, "I am gay."

"There are times when the world kind of screeches to a halt, and everything rearranges itself backwards to forwards and up and down, and this was one of those times. I said to Howard, 'You're gay?' 'Yes' said Howard, 'I am gay.'

When the world stopped rearranging itself I said, 'Oh!' Howard started telling me a little bit about his wife, the troubles he had in Wisconsin, the reasons he came to Coos Bay, the problems with his wife leading to their eventual separation. It was quite a long talk. When we were done, I bid him good-bye.

"I left the day care center early that day and wandered down to the pizza shop and had myself a beer. When I was done with that I had myself another beer. I was trying to put it all together. It was just too amazing. It was too beyond the pale. Things like this only happened in soap operas. While I was sitting there, who should wander in but Howard. He sat down again. I really didn't want to see Howard right then because I was too busy rearranging Coos Bay. Nonetheless, he sat down and continued telling me things about his life.

"And I guess I have one more thing to say about Howard. The whole thing that happened, happened in Coos Bay, the logger capital of the Western Hemisphere, a city so conservative that Christian wasn't enough, and born-again Christian was necessary for admission to most circles; for you to tell the church, first that you didn't believe in God and thought you had been sold a bill of goods, and then later on that you were gay, was something out of any overworked scriptwriter's mind, and I could never quite believe that it really happened. I am glad that you are writing the story about it."

That was a nice letter, but I had come to Coos Bay to meet with those people who were still living in Coos Bay and had stayed through the thick and thin of that journey. They had let me know they wanted to meet with me. They were not writers and could not put their feelings in words, but felt they would be able to express themselves if I met with them. I also liked the idea. It would give me a chance to find out if the sermons and the teaching in the adult groups had any impact.

The gathering was very much like any of the adult study groups which had been so important in the life of the congregation. There was a slight difference. Only a few came for dinner, and the rest arrived for desert. As they arrived it was like old home week. The fifteen years were but a moment and we picked up where we had left off. Oh, the bodies had changed, but the persons were the same. After the chitchat was over, I turned on my tape recorder and asked, "Why did you stay when all the others left?"

Eleanor: "I remember you telling us, when we tried to define God, we put a limit to God. I have remembered that, thought about it and thought about it. So you did teach me something."

Vera: "I was here first, but you gave me a challenge. You said, 'I don't expect you to agree with me, but I do expect you to think.' It wasn't your theology that attracted me. It was that challenge."

Eleanor: "He would say, 'Go in peace,' and I would say, 'How can we, when you preach that kind of sermon?'"

Lillian: "I joined the church, not the minister. But I remember you had a sermon once that God could be found in a tavern, or anywhere."

Kate: "There was the challenge. I remember telling you one time that you were hard on us. You made us go home thinking and talking to ourselves. I felt I learned more about religion from your sermons and your conversations. I had passed the time when a person at church got a pat on their head and the words, 'go home and be a good little girl and everything will be okay.' If it wasn't, what happened? Everything was negative. I couldn't find it. I questioned the God-He, the Personified One-up-there. I had an awful time with that. I always had a hard time with that. I thought, 'There must be something wrong with me. I'm a good Christian person.' You kinda of knocked that out of my head, and that got me started on the right road. I had felt I was the odd one out since I did not believe in a God-up-there pulling strings, changing His mind, that kind of thing. If negative things happened to me, then I wondered, "What have I done?" I felt strange thinking that way, but your teaching validated my questioning the traditional approach."

Kate continued in another direction: "And the idea of prayer. I have come to the point where prayer to me is a feeling I have. I do not mouth any words. It is just feeling. I cannot put my thoughts into words, but then I am beginning to think that is a prayer."

Elaine: "I stayed because I liked your sermons. They stimulated me. You opened up the idea of freedom as I always thought it should be. It did not matter whether I agreed with you or not. It caused me to think and led me to realize that I could feel a lot freer to associate with fundamentalists, or people who were totally different religiously. I no longer felt threatened. I was secure in what I believed. I used to feel threatened. When I was young we went to a Baptist church, and people went forward. I did not want to go forward, and I would feel terrible about that. I'd go home and cry, feeling I was a bad girl because I didn't go forward. I just could not do that. There was something about me which said that I should do that. Then I would ask myself, 'Why should I do that? I'm a Christian and I do not have to do that.' Anyway it opened a freedom from that approach and moved into other areas of my life."

Dave: " I think back to my involvement in the church as a young man in high school. I went off to college and into the military, and when I came back I was returning to my home church. What I had remembered was the Oscar Payne era. (My predecessor) I came out of the army as a lst lieutenant. I had been in Korea. I had been in Alabama. The worst part of the war was being in the Ozarks.

When I returned home I'll never forget the first Sunday. During my years in college and the army, I had not been involved in any church. The first month or so after my return I would leave on a Sunday morning shaking my head with this radical. All I remember was my childhood. But your sermons included statements which questioned our involvement in Vietnam. I was really wrestling with those issues. I had not been very comfortable in the army because I kept thinking about them. I listened carefully to what you were saying and realized that you were voicing many of the ideas I had been thinking but did not know how to verbalize. It took a few months, almost a year in fact, before I realized the reason for my discomfort in the military.

Dave continued: "For the first time in my life, I began to think more in global terms. The experience we had caused me to think about more than Coos Bay. I had a narrow tunnel vision of the world even though I had been in the military and college. I began to see that there were other people to care about. As I have thought about it the last twenty-five years, one of the reasons I became involved was your preaching. Leaving the service on Sunday, not having been comforted, led me to think and to extend myself more than I would have otherwise. I think it was the process, the wrestling, the challenge. If I had not had that experience, which developed a caring for people, I am not sure I would have become involved down the road."

Len: "I frequently wondered where would we be, the people in this room, where would the world be, where would the subject of theology be without the 'God is dead' theology which you gave us. I am speaking in national and international terms. We (he and his family) were attracted to you by what you were preaching and by knowing you. We came out of a fundamental church in which I had spent my life. You may remember the minister of that church being hatched for being liberal. When he left we came to the Presbyterian church.

"It was important to me, and I think it might have been important to others in that group of men who met with you once a week to study *Honest to God.* The sessions were held in the Elk's Lodge. That book made a big change in my life, and you were the one who helped me understand what was in the book. I had not been a great scholar of the new theology, but those sessions helped me at an important time in my life.

"I know another individual who was going through the same struggle. Unfortunately he did not find a place to land and has been unchurched since. I think this is the down side of this whole matter. The church has not picked up, the church has not listened. They have not followed through on the liberalism, the freedom you talked about. I wanted to believe what Paul wrote, that in Christ we were free. We had no freedom in the church we were in. From that time on we (he and his wife) have been on a journey and are still on a journey, and we don't ever expect to finish in this life. We are continually pressing onward, and it got its start at that period of time in our lives, and you were one of the catalysts."

Prior to the meeting I had sent the first draft of the first section of the book which some of the people had had a chance to read before this meeting.

Joyce: "'That Sunday' you talk about in the beginning, were you preaching sermons along that line before?"

"I had been hinting, " I replied, "but not to the point that I had attacked the doctrine of God. By the time you came, I had been attacking much of traditional Protestant concepts. I had spoken to one of the service clubs, and at a few other places."

Joyce: "We knew of your reputation. That's why we came."

Vera: "Everybody in town knew of your sermons."

I interjected, "I think one of the confessions I must make to all of you is that after I left Coos Bay, I had to live what I had preached. That was not part of the contract of being a minister." Laughter. "I began to understand what I had expected of you and now had to face myself."

Kate: "Maybe you were a positive experience for us."

211

Someone said, "Maybe?"

Laughter.

"Yes," I replied. "In John's Gospel when Nathaniel was introduced to Jesus, he said, 'What good can come out of Nazareth?' I have thought about that many times and said to myself, 'What good can come out of Coos Bay?'"

"My grandson came to visit," said Eleanor, "and apparently I mentioned that you were gay. He responded, 'It doesn't matter. I like him.'"

Phyllis: "Do you think this was a good place to bring this out? Did anybody help you at this point in your life in Coos Bay? Did you have anybody you felt comfortable with? I mean after you told us?"

"Yes," I replied. "Ed was here."

The sections of Good Friday and Easter had not been written at the time of the meeting, so in response to the question from Phyllis, I shared with them my experience with the minister at the workshop on worship and my affair with Anthony.

Dave said, "There were a couple of events that helped me in terms of accepting people. I, like most of the people in the church, was going on my merry way, and Howard first announced the divorce, and then that he was gay. Knowing Howard and liking him as a minister with all the talent he had was no reason for me to turn the church or Howard off just because he was gay. It also caused me to be more accepting of a whole variety of differences in people. Had I not known Howard, I think I might have handled it differently. Knowing someone and then learning something about that person's lifestyle was a help."

I responded, "Sometime after the divorce, when I was putting my life together, I was visited by Dave. He was concerned that my preaching had slipped greatly. I had been aware of that for a couple of years and seemed a bit helpless to do anything about it.

212

Part of my problem was that I was going through male menopause at that same time."

Laughter.

"It was a very low time in my life and the experience with those two men, but my relationship with Anthony in particular, helped keep me going."

Jay: "For me the gayness was a very minor side issue. Part of my problem was, I knew nothing of what was going on. For me the importance of your ministry was not the gay issue. It was only an interesting aspect of my Coos Bay experience. When I was away from Coos Bay I could brag to my friends that I had a minister who was gay, but as far as its being important to what I was getting out of the Presbyterian experience, it had no relevance at all. What I remember were the sermons on pertinent issues that were occurring on a day-to-day basis, books I had read, movies I had experienced, and I think Star Trek. I'm beginning to see more of what you were seeing in them."

Like most of the group meetings during my ministry, after the original discussion had more or less run its course, the conversation often took off into related areas or something totally different. This was true of this meeting as well. Those in the group who had read the first draft of the first section began to give me some pointers on improving it. Jay had voiced an objection that I had started with the sexual.

I replied, "I started with the sexual because the struggle for me began with the sexual, and what I had done was against my religious upbringing. It is there at the beginning of the book to help the straight world have some understanding of the difficult internal struggle gay people have in coming to terms with their sexuality. I think the struggle is even more difficult for gays and lesbians who want to be involved in a church. There are many homosexual people who do not make it and, in the struggle of coming to terms with their sexuality, turn to alcohol or drugs. It may not be important to you, but the sexual parts are there to help gays and lesbians know they do not have to live a lie. At least in the church they should be able to come out. But it is the church which continues to condemn them for their lifestyle. If all the homosexual clergy who are serving the institutional church would stand up, the church would shake to its very foundations.

"After I had come out in 1977, other homosexual Presbyterian ministers were aware of what I had done, and they watched to see what would happen to me. When they read what happened after I left Coos Bay, they all stayed in the closet. What is more interesting is that the national Presbyterian organization concerned with homosexual issues, ordination, and the homophobia in the Presbyterian church, also ignored me. What I had done in Coos Bay apparently made no impression on their leadership. Evidently they too, could not believe any good could come out of Coos Bay. I am still ignored by that organization to this day."

Eleanor: "I think you got the shaft."

"That's beside the point, " I replied. "In a conversation with me, a fellow Presbyterian minister said, 'You are twenty years ahead of our time,' and I responded, 'You mean you do not want to deal with me.' The crucifixion I faced from the Presbyterian ministers in the Presbytery after leaving Coos Bay was worse than anything I had confronted in Coos Bay. When I needed help, none offered any. In fact, when I confronted one minister about this lack of support, he replied, 'You are such a strong person, I did not think you needed any help.' This from a minister who built his ministry on counseling people. I had been part of the power structure of the Presbytery and felt this would have been a help when it came time for me to have to leave Coos Bay, but the staff person for the Ministerial Relations Division of the Presbytery made sure I did not have a chance at another church. This information came to me from another staff member some years after I left Coos Bay . I learned that I had been blackballed in California, and my dossier was not allowed to be given to any vacant church for consideration.

I continued, "The hurt and anger I felt toward the Presbytery lasted for a long time. But the day I attended the meeting of Presbytery where I would be retired, I went in peace. I had forgiven them. The suffering and the pain I had experienced after leaving Coos Bay was necessary for me. I would not have grown as I have, had I not faced that death, so that Easter could come. What I had preached to you, I finally had to live in my own life."

Velva: "Why did they honorably retire you? Did they have a record of the fact, or did you ask for retirement? How did it come about?"

"I asked for it," I replied.

"You asked to be retired?" asked Velva.

"Yes," was my reply. "I was planning on selling my business, so I wanted to be retired by the Presbytery to qualify for my pension. I asked to be retired. They put the 'honorable' designation on my retirement."

"As of what date?" asked Jay.

"Oh, this was almost five years ago, about 1987."

"But there was no ministry for you between 1977 and then?"

I said, "I had prepared several ministries for gays and lesbians at the request of the Presbytery and waited for an answer. Finally the chairman of the Ministerial Relations Committee called me and said that I had to have some kind of non-parish ministry that the Presbytery could approve. I told him that I had submitted three different proposals for a ministry to gays and lesbians. He seemed surprised and said, 'They must have gotten lost in committee.' 'Are you kidding?' I responded, and chided him for making such a remark. I reminded him that I had been a member of the committee which had developed the procedure for validating non-parish ministries, and said, 'Proposals do not get lost in committees.'"

Jay responded, "You mean when you left here you made three proposals, all lost in committee?"

"Yes," I answered. "I could understand their losing the one which involved money. But the others. No Way! I had also told the staff person for Ministerial Relations that I was interested in being a stated supply. He made sure I did not function in any capacity in any church."

"So you have not been in a pulpit since you left?" asked Jay.

"I have been a guest preacher only twice, but the chance of being a pastor was denied, and I was also prevented from being considered as a stated supply."

Eleanor interrupted the conversation and asked, "Howard, I want to ask you something. Do you think that almost everyone somewhere in their life or someplace inside themselves has a tendency toward homosexuality?"

"Yes, and No," was my immediate response. "If sex is kept strictly on a physical level many people can go both ways."

"Can one go both ways, or either way?" she asked.

"Most people know where it's at when they first begin to think about sex or begin to become sexually active," was my response. "When I am talking about being gay I am not just talking about two bodies meeting and enjoying sex."

"I understand that," said Eleanor.

"I'm talking about a mind-set," I continued. "I'm talking about the inner me. I am talking about myself. Being gay has to do with the total person. I am convinced we are a third sex. We are a unisex. We are both in one. Not only do I have to deal with being gay, as a male I have to deal with the femininity which is within me. This is more than being a sensitive, kind, considerate, nurturing person. These attributes are not restricted to women. Any person can have them. By the same token Lesbians have to deal with their masculinity. We have to come to terms with the fact we are a unisex, and then whatever kind of body (male or female) we are in is the direction our sexuality takes."

"That is where its supposed to be directed?" asked Eleanor.

"Yes," I replied. "If we do not go in the right direction we are in for all kinds of trouble. It is in the sexual act that gays and lesbians encounter where their sexuality is complete. It is also where we experience being both male and female. Unfortunately only a few of the more serious minds within the gay community have talked much about our being unisex, but it is a dilemma with which we have to deal. In my case I think both sides are quite even. When I moved to Portland, I began to allow the femininity to come into its own."

Len asked, "Could you have had the theology without the sexuality?"

"I do not think so," was my reply.

"You don't think so?" responded Len. "You think it is impossible for a heterosexual to come up with what you did?"

"I am not saying it is impossible," I responded. "But as a straight person you would come to it from a different direction. As I have indicated, a person's spirituality and sexuality do go hand in hand. Of all the areas in which life is lived, it is in the realm of the sexual that we have been given the greatest freedom, and therefore, the greatest temptations for wrong use. When Yahweh breathed into that piece of clay, we became living beings with freedom. It is in the realm of the physical sexual act that all aspects of any human being – physical, mental and spiritual – can come together. When this happens we can be taken into an experience beyond our expectation and comprehension, a truly spiritual experience. The greater the freedom, the greater the temptation. Our spirituality is the area of the greatest freedom, and how we use that freedom is critical to our total being as persons."

I continued, "I think for heterosexuals this relationship between the sexual and spiritual is even more subtle. Your sexuality is taken for granted, but is too often seen as separate from the rest of your life. As a member of the Ministerial Relations Committee in several Presbyteries, I learned that most often it was the most religious, most pious minister who was playing around with the women in his congregation. In recent years two well-known television evangelists were doing the same thing. So from my perspective, our spirituality and our sexuality do go hand in hand. I never heard any minister suggest the two went together. But this has been my experience. My greatest frustrations and

217

temptations as well as my greatest joys and pleasures have been sexual."

The conversation turned in another direction. It concerned promiscuity. I had made the statement that I could not resist a man who attracted me, anymore than a straight man could resist a woman who attracted him.

Len asked, "Is there more promiscuity among gay men than in the so-called straight world?"

"Not from what I knew went on in Coos Bay, " I replied. "The straight world covered it up. They did not talk about it."

Len continued, "Payton Place was the whole rage in that day. All that was happening in the show was taking place in Coos Bay."

"And still is," interjected Phyllis.

"And they talk about it on the talk shows," added Linda.

"If the soap operas are any indication of what life is all about," I said, "we gay people are no worse. I think there are some differences in the realm of sexuality. Gay men are more free to engage in impersonal sex because we can more easily divorce the act from the emotional. We can keep it strictly on the physical because everything hangs out. Our primary sexual organ is outside, and we shoot out the life giving substance when we ejaculate. This is also true for straight men and is an explanation for why straight men see women as sexual objects who are around for their pleasure.

"For women the primary sexual organ is inside. This makes sex more internal for them, and they must be more in control of their bodies than men. That is why women have a very different mind set in regard to sex. As a gay man I have experienced both aspects, which enables me to understand women to some degree. Another reason gay men can more easily engage in impersonal sex is that they do not have to worry about becoming pregnant. Straight people do. Many gay men engage in impersonal sex as an escape from commitment, and if they want to settle for that they get their just rewards: no real satisfaction, no fulfillment of love."

218

I continued, "The straight world does the same. There are baths were straights can go and have sex with anyone there. Couple-swapping groups are available, and in those situations I would think the sex would be quite impersonal. It seems to me that often in impersonal sex, people are really looking for intimacy and not just sex. They get the two mixed up. Intimacy is the larger context in which sex takes place, finds its ultimate meaning, and that is where it should be."

"It's the bonding agent," said Len, and the rest of the group nodded in agreement.

I responded that it seemed to me that people who say that friendship is not the basis of a marriage are missing the boat.

Len said, "We know two couples quite well, guys who have been together for years and probably will die together, and it seems to me they have so much more than what I visualized."

"There is no question in my mind," I replied, "that it is the same in the homosexual world and in the heterosexual."

Phyllis added, "It's companionship. I'm wondering what's happening to the young teenagers, the boys who are going through this?"

Elaine, who had taught music in school, answered, "Well, I know at school, if the kids thought someone might be gay they really crucified them. Sometimes I would get to school early, and they would forget I was there, and they would really give someone they thought might be gay a bad time. I'm like you Len, I didn't think too much about it. I just thought, 'Oh well.' I remember two boys. I really liked both of them. They had a lot going for them. One was well-adjusted in high school, but the other was kinda out of it."

Linda asked, "If you found Mr. Wonderful, would that not be different? If you had a relationship that was right, would you be able to resist other men?"

"Yes," I replied. "When I have been involved with another man, I discovered that other men had lost their appeal. I have met gay men whose relationship has lasted until death did them part."

219

The discussion changed once again. They talked about the members who had left the congregation.

Lillian said, "They left not because of your homosexuality; it was your theology. A lot of them left because they did not want to be challenged."

"That's right," added Len. "Salvation and redemptive theology was really very easy. Jesus did it all. All we had to do was follow a bunch of rules which the church had set up. Anything more was too much."

"They didn't want to think," said Lillian.

"I guess they wanted to be told," was my response, "and when I changed it to everyone taking responsibility for all the good and evil we do, then we were in a totally different ball game."

Another member wrote:

NO CHURCH PICNIC

As the service came to a close
wife, son and daughter by his side
he rose, "Now that our children
are grown, we want you to know
our marriage has come to an end.
I am the cause, not she, of the lie
we have lived for them.

No one there that Sunday morning
could imagine being as brave.
Those who loved him stood firm.
Those who did not hissed him out
with small town venom.
In the big city
he joined a church of pariahs
free at last to say, "I am gay."

Since then ten years have passed.
Son and daughter visit often.
Their mother is happy in a new marriage.

He, retired from the rigors
of janitor labor, hones his musical skills
and ministers to his dying brothers..
I wonder if he knows
his ministry lives on in us.

Celia Piehl

The next day as I was returning to Portland that bright light in the back of my head came on once more. All these years I had been upset with Presbytery for having destroyed what I had accomplished in that church. Once again it dawned on me that what had happened was very much like what happened in the New Testament. Not long after the Easter event the disciples and followers broke up and went their separate ways. So also with the members of the Coos Bay Presbyterian Church. Many left and went their separate ways sharing their new lives with others.

A GLOSSARY OF PRESBYTERIAN TERMS

General Assembly: The General Assembly is the highest of the four governing bodies in the Presbyterian Church (U.S.A.)

Synod: The Synod is the middle governing body made up of presbytery representatives.

Presbytery: The Presbytery is the governing body composed of churches within a geographical boundary.

Session: The Session is the governing body of a local church composed of the Minister, who is the moderator, and members of the congregation elected by the members.

Governing Bodies: Session, presbytery, synod and General Assembly.

Moderator: Presiding officer of a committee, youth group, board of deacons, session, presbytery, synod, or General Assembly. Moderators serve a one-year term of office.

Elders: Persons elected by the congregation to serve on the Session. Elders are ordained to the office of elder.

Stated Clerk: Secretary-parliamentarian at the levels of presbytery, synod, and General Assembly.

Ordination: Ordination is the setting apart for the ministry of the Word or the office of elder or deacon. Person are ordained only once.

Deacons: A group of persons with specific tasks granted by the session to the members of the congregation.

Delegate/Commissioner: Delegate: any person delegated to a specific task. Commissioner: minister or elder elected to a governing body.

Candidates: Students preparing for the ministry who have been approved by the presbytery as candidates under the care of presbytery.

Book of Order: Contains (1) Form of Government, (2) Rules of Discipline, (3) Directory for the Service of God (worship guidelines.)

Rules of Discipline: Section of the Book of Order relating to church discipline and conflict resolution.

Trustees: Legally elected managers of a corporation. The Office ordinarily relates to matters of property. Many Presbyterian churches now have a unicameral system of government which means sessions serve concurrently as boards of trustees.

FOOTNOTES

Reminiscences
    1. Matt. 4:10

That Sunday
    1. Matt. 12:24-26

A Brave Beginning
    1. I Kings 19:9-18

A New Culture
    1. John Wick Bowman, *The Intention of Jesus,* p.219f.

Walking on Water
    1. Matt. 14:28,29
    2. Matt. 16:25
    3. Matt. 19:16-22

Adrift
    1. Matt. 5:44-47
    2. Matt. 22:36,37
    3. Matt. 5:44-47

The Shadow of the Cross
    1. Mark 10:25
    2. Mark 10:29f
    3. Luke 15:11-32

Death & Dying
    1. Romans 12:1-2

Another Mr. Wonderful
    1. John 4:23-25

A Ray of Light
    1. Matt. 8:36
Some Thoughts from the Gospel of John
    1. John 20:25
    2. John 20:28, 29
    3. John 8:31, 32
    4. John 6:35
    5. John 8:12
    6. John 14:6

Final Days
    1. Eze. 16:49, 50
    2. Judges 19:16-18
    3. Luke 10:12, 13
    4. Lev. 18:22; 20:13
    5. Romans 1:26, 27
    6. Gal. 3:28
    7. John 1:1, 11, 12